AF579973

Race, Performance, and Approval of Mayors

List of Previous Publications

Susan E. Howell

2006

with Alicia Jencik. "'I Can't Imagine It': Survey Research in Post-Katrina New Orleans." *Public Opinion Pros: An Online Magazine for the Polling Professional (and Everybody Else)*. October. Available at http://www.publicopinionpros.com.

2004

with Huey L. Perry. "Black Mayors / White Mayors: Explaining Their Approval." *Public Opinion Quarterly* 68 (Spring): 32–57.

with Huey L. Perry, and Matthew A. Vile. "Black Cities / White Cities: Evaluating the Police." *Political Behavior* 6 (March): 45–68.

2002

"Against the Tide." *The Polling Report* 18, no. 24 (December 23): 1–5. Invited.

"Race and Gender as Cues for Blacks and Whites: A Survey-Based Experiment." *The American Review of Politics* 23 (Fall/Winter): 275–86.

2001

with Sara C. Benesh. "Confidence in the Courts: A Comparison of Users and Non-Users." *Behavioral Sciences and the Law* 19, no. 2:199–214.

with William McLean. "Performance and Race in Evaluating Minority Mayors." *Public Opinion Quarterly* 65 (Fall): 321–43.

2000

"Racial Polarization and the Reaction to Urban Conditions." In *Black and Multi-Racial Politics in America*, edited by Yvette Alex-Assenoh and Lawrence Hanks, 60–83. New York: New York University Press.

with Christine L. Day. "Complexities of the Gender Gap." *The Journal of Politics* 62, no. 3 (August): 858–74.

1998

with Brent Marshall. "Crime and Trust in Local Government: Revisiting a Black Empowerment Zone." *Urban Affairs Review* 33, no. 3 (January): 361–81.

1996

with Lyle Downing. "David Duke: Democracy under Stress in Louisiana." In *Research on Democracy and Society*, edited by Frederick Weil, 177–95. Greenwich, CT: JAI Press.

1994

"Racism, Cynicism, Economics and David Duke." *American Politics Quarterly* 22 (April) 190–207.

with Robert T. Sims. "Survey Research and Racially Charged Elections." *Political Behavior* 16 (June): 219–36.

1993

with Anton Pelinka. "Duke and Haider: Right-Wing Politics in Comparison." *Contemporary Austrian Studies* 2:152–71.

with Robert T. Sims. "Abortion Attitudes and the Louisiana Governor's Election." *American Politics Quarterly* 21 (January): 54–64. Also published in *Understanding the New Politics of Abortion*, edited by Malcolm Goggin, 154–62. Newbury Park, CA: Sage.

1992

with Shirley B. Laska. "The Changing Face of the Environmental Coalition." *Environment and Behavior* 24, no. 1 (January): 134–44.

with Sylvia Warren. "Public Opinion and David Duke." In *The David Duke Controversy*, edited by Douglas Rose, 80–93. Chapel Hill: University of North Carolina Press. Named "Outstanding Book on the Subject of Human Rights" by the Gustavus Myers Center.

1991

"Who Voted for David Duke?" *The Polling Report* 7, no. 24 (December): 1–8. Invited.

1990

with Deborah Fagan. "Race and Trust in Government: Testing the Political Reality Model." *Public Opinion Quarterly* 52, no. 3 (Fall): 343–50.

with James Vanderleeuw. "Economic Effects on State Governors." *American Politics Quarterly* 18 (April): 158–68.

with James M. Vanderleeuw. "A Social Cleavage Model of Ideological Identification." *Southeastern Political Review* 18, no. 2 (Fall): 1–15.

1988

"Candidates and Issues in Local Elections." *American Politics Quarterly* 16, no. 1 (January): 25–42.

1986

"Candidates and Attitudes: The Question of Causality Revisited." *Journal of Politics* 48, no. 2 (May): 450–64.

1985

"Chasing An Elusive Concept: Ideological Identifications and Presidential Elections." *Political Behavior* 7, no. 4:325–34.

1984

with Stephen Hayes, Steven Shull, and John Flaxbeard. "Presidential Support Among Senatorial Leaders and Followers." *American Politics Quarterly* 12 (April): 195–209.

1983

with Michael D. McDonald. "Reconsidering the Reconceptualizations of Party Identification." *Political Methodology* 8, no. 4:73–91.

1982

with William S. Oiler. "Campaign Activities and Local Election Outcomes." *Social Science Quarterly* 62, no. 1 (March): 151–60.

1981

"Short Term Forces and Changing Partisanship." *Political Behavior* 3, no. 2:163–80.

1980

"The Behavioral Component of Changing Partisanship." *American Politics Quarterly* 8 (July): 279–302.

"Local Election Campaigns: The Effects of Office Level on Campaign Style." *Journal of Politics* 42, no. 4 (November): 1135–45.

with Charles D. Hadley. "The Southern Split Ticket Voter, 1952–1976: Republican Conversion or Democratic Decline?" In *Party Politics in The South*, edited by Robert Steed, Lawrence Moreland, and Told Baker, 127–51. New York: Praeger.

1979

"Local Party Activities and the Psychological Dimension of Unity in American Parties." *Journal of the Georgia Political Science Association* 7, no. 2 (Fall): 1–21.

with Charles D. Hadley. "Partisan Conversion in the Northeast: An Analysis of Split Ticket Voting, 1952–1975." *American Politics Quarterly* 7 (July): 259–82.

with William S. Oiler. "Evaluations of Presidential Policy Performance." In *The Presidency: Studies in Policy Making*, edited by Steven A. Shull and Lance LeLoup, 47–64. Brunswick, OH: King's Court Communications.

1976

"Political Information: The Effects of System and Individual Characteristics." *Comparative Political Studies* 8, no. 4 (January): 413–35.

Race, Performance, and Approval of Mayors

Susan E. Howell

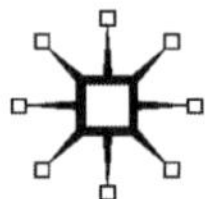

RACE, PERFORMANCE, AND APPROVAL OF MAYORS

First published in 2007 by
PALGRAVE MACMILLAN™
175 Fifth Avenue, New York, N.Y. 10010 and
Houndmills, Basingstoke, Hampshire, England RG21 6XS.
Companies and representatives throughout the world.

PALGRAVE MACMILLAN is the global academic imprint of the Palgrave Macmillan division of St. Martin's Press, LLC and of Palgrave Macmillan Ltd. Macmillan® is a registered trademark in the United States, United Kingdom and other countries. Palgrave is a registered trademark in the European Union and other countries.

ISBN-13: 978–1–4039–7459–4
ISBN-10: 1–4039–7459–4

Library of Congress Cataloging-in-Publication Data

Howell, Susan E.
Race, performance, and approval of mayors / Susan E. Howell.
p. cm.
Includes bibliographical references and index.
ISBN 1–4039–7459–4
1. Mayors—United States—Case studies. 2. African American mayors—Public opinion—Case studies. 3. United States—Race relations—Case studies. I. Title.
JS356.H69 2006
320.8'54—dc22 2006048210

A catalogue record of the book is available from the British Library.

Design by Scribe Inc.

First edition: January 2007

10 9 8 7 6 5 4 3 2 1

Printed in the United States of America.

Dedicated to my husband, John, my son, Matt, and the graduate students of the University of New Orleans Survey Research Center.

Table of Contents

List of Figures and Tables

Figures

Tables

Preface

This research examines how performance and race interweave to affect mayoral approval in four cities, two are majority black with black mayors, and two are majority white with white mayors. The project was inspired by twenty years of conducting Quality of Life surveys in New Orleans, LA. Throughout those studies three patterns emerged: the concept of "quality of life" at the local level is quite complex, there are racial differences in perceptions of the quality of life, and the mayor suffers or gains as perceptions of the quality of life improve or deteriorate. There is a wealth of existing research on presidential approval, and a modest amount on approval of governors. Most of this research is based on a performance model whereby the president or governor is rewarded or punished by perceptions of his performance. Oddly, this model has rarely been extended down to the third level of executive office, mayors. Moreover, because of the increasing number of African American mayors and majority minority cities, race may be a confounding factor in the operation of the performance model in racially diverse settings. The rise of black political empowerment at the local level provides an opportunity to study how race complicates the performance model.

List of Contributors

Ronald H. Bayor

Professor of History, Technology and Society, Georgia Institute of Technology. He is a historian who specializes in urban, ethnic and immigration history. He is the founding editor of Journal of American Ethnic History and served as editor from 1981–2004. He is author of *Neighbors in Conflict: The Irish, Germans, Jews, and Italians of New York City, 1929–1941* (Choice outstanding academic book for 1978); *Fiorello LaGuardia: Ethnicity and Reform*; and *Race and the Shaping of Twentieth-Century Atlanta* (outstanding book award from the Gustavus Myers Center for the Study of Human Rights in North America). He is also coauthor of *Engineering the New South: Georgia Tech 1885–1985*; editor of *Neighborhoods in Urban America*; co-editor of *The New York Irish* (James S. Donnelly, Sr. prize of the American Conference for Irish Studies for best book in history and social sciences), and editor of *Race and Ethnicity in America: A Concise History* and *The Columbia Documentary History of Race and Ethnicity in America.*

Huey L. Perry

Professor and Chancellor's Fellow in Political Science at Southern University, Baton Rouge, LA. He specializes in racial politics, race and elections, and the concept of deracialization. He is author of numerous articles on African American mayors in the south, particularly Richard Arrington of Birmingham and Dutch Morial of New Orleans. He edited *Race, Politics and Governance in the United States*. He has also published articles on mayoral approval and on the relationship between blacks and the police.

Acknowledgments

This research is a collaborative effort of many people—graduate students, colleagues, family members, and reviewers—who have contributed numerous suggestions, criticisms, and helpful insights. To begin with, I am grateful to historian Ronald H. Bayor who authored two chapters providing historical background on African American mayors and these four cities in particular. Political scientist Huey L. Perry also contributed to one of the historical chapters. The project was funded by the National Science Foundation, and I am grateful to Frank Scioli for his suggestions during the submission phase. The surveys themselves were conducted at the University of New Orleans Survey Research Center, and I want to thank the graduate students who contributed conceptually, as well as by working nights and weekends on this project: Matthew Vile, Heidi Unter, Monica Farris, and Manabu Saeki. The anonymous Palgrave reviewer made many helpful suggestions which improved the final product. Finally, my husband, John, was unfailingly supportive and provided much technical assistance; I would not have persisted to finish this project without him.

During Hurricane Katrina, the Survey Research Center and the Political Science Department at the University of New Orleans were both heavily damaged. Recovery will be slow, but I will always be grateful to my colleagues and the graduate students who, for thirty years, created a stimulating environment for teaching and research.

Chapter 1
Performance Models and Mayoral Approval

All elected executives—presidents, governors, and mayors—seek approval from their constituencies. Even though these officials may deny its importance, they almost universally realize that citizen approval is a kind of political capital, which can be enhanced or squandered. Approval ratings are a running tally of how citizens view their elected leaders. A number of political actors carefully watch ratings to judge the range of possibility in political activity. An executive with high approval ratings will find it easier to succeed with the legislature because individual legislators will be reluctant to defy a popular executive. An elected official with high approval ratings will also find it easier to deal with the bureaucracy since individual members of the bureaucracy will perceive the executive as having support for his or her policies. On the other hand, if approval ratings are low or dropping, the executive will find that opponents in the legislature are more aggressive, while supporters are hard to find. Also, in negotiating with the bureaucracy, individual department heads and others will feel freer to make decisions on their own, knowing that the executive's authority is weakened. In sum, approval simply makes governing easier.

Probably the most famous running tallies of executive approval are the ubiquitous presidential approval ratings put forth by national survey organizations, such as Gallup, CBS/*New York Times*, and ABC/*Washington Post*. These numbers are not just presented as raw figures. Nearly every week, the media, public officials, and politically interested citizens analyze these numbers. Approval ratings have a half-life, or echo effect, that permeates discussion of the impact of presidential actions. The president, members of Congress, members of the bureaucracy, state officials, and numerous other actors interpret these approval ratings to the president's advantage or detriment.

One of the best examples of the power of presidential approval ratings occurred during the Clinton impeachment crisis of 1998. Throughout the disclosures, hearings, and even after the vote to impeach, sixty percent of the public continued to approve of the president's performance, and two-thirds opposed his removal from office. Republicans in Congress and elsewhere watched in vain for a drop in the president's approval ratings. Democrats, too, followed the polls, partly to estimate the political wisdom of standing by the president. The "firewall" of Clinton's approval ratings sent a consistent message to both parties—the public considered removal from office a disproportionate response to the president's transgressions. Of course, record economic growth was the primary reason for Clinton's popularity, but, given the deluge of negative publicity, it is astonishing that his approval ratings were not damaged. Ultimately, impeachment never went beyond the House of Representatives because there was simply not enough support in the Senate. Thus, there is a good argument to be made that approval ratings saved Bill Clinton's presidency.

Most of the existing research on executive approval ratings is based on a performance model that emphasizes citizen evaluations of conditions in the country or state, most commonly economic. There is ample evidence that economic evaluations directly affect presidential and gubernatorial popularity. Evaluations of economic and other aspects of performance also influence voting for or against an incumbent executive. While this latter research has focused on voting as a dependent variable, it is easy to see the applicability to approval of incumbents.

The key theoretical question in this research is whether the performance model of executive approval applies to the local level. Oddly, this model has rarely been extended down to the third level of executive office: mayors. Consistent with the research on national and state executive approval, a city's economy can be one basis for judging mayoral performance. However, there are other sentiments about conditions in the city that could also serve as evaluations of performance. Citizens can evaluate cities in terms of crime control, street conditions, housing, parks, public transportation, and schools. In addition, these aspects of urban life can be closely observed in the course of daily life, in contrast to conditions in the state or the nation. Thus, it is reasonable to expect that the performance model of approval could apply to mayors as well as to presidents and governors.

However, there is a major complication to applying the performance model at the local level. Every U.S. president and governor since the Reconstruction has been white, with the exception of Governor L. Douglas Wilder of Virginia. Moving to the local level introduces black executives into the mix. These officials have been studied largely in terms of racial politics, and because of the increasing number of African American mayors and cities where people of color are the majority, race may be a confounding factor in the operation of the performance model in these racially diverse settings.

The rise of black political empowerment at the local level provides an opportunity to study executive approval while taking into account both the race of the executive and the race of the constituents. Factors that influence approval of black mayors can be compared to the factors influencing approval of their white counterparts. Cities that elect black mayors are often plagued by dwindling jobs, white flight, poor schools, crime, and deteriorating housing (Reed 1988; Barnes 1994; Nelson 1990; Preston 1990; Kraus and Swanstrom 2001). However, there is little systematic research on the consequences of black mayors' effectiveness in dealing with these problems. In their study of New Orleans, Susan E. Howell and William McLean found that performance had greater explanatory power over approval of the African American mayor than racial factors, but the finding was based on only one year of study (Howell and McLean 2001). Overall, there has been little systematic research on black *or* white mayoral approval.

In addition to addressing the theoretical question of the performance model, there are implications for governance and legitimacy. Some cities have had black mayors for more than twenty years, which should have reduced their novelty. If these mayors still are evaluated more in terms of race than performance, it is a sad conclusion for urban race relations. A racial evaluation complicates governance for black mayors who often have to negotiate with a white racial minority who controls a disproportionately large amount of the city's wealth. On the other hand, if performance has become the primary yardstick for evaluating both black and white mayors, then urban residents are perhaps becoming less sensitive to race in evaluating urban officials (see Moesher and Silver 1994; Sonenshein 1989; Hajnal 2004). In these cases the mayor gains or loses legitimacy biracially, based on citizens' evaluation of performance.

There are also implications for creating and maintaining a racially diverse city. Maintaining that racial balance is partially dependent on having biracial support for the mayor's public policies, a situation that is difficult under conditions of severe racial polarization. Black mayors will have a more difficult task than white mayors in this effort if race and racial attitudes drive mayoral approval. However, if the citizens' approval of a black mayor is performance based, then black mayors who succeed in improving conditions may be able to diminish white flight and maintain a healthy racial balance.

How much is mayoral approval in racially diverse cities influenced by race and racial attitudes? How much is mayoral approval influenced by citizen evaluations of conditions in the city, or performance? Is the relative influence of these two factors different for white mayors and black mayors? These are some of the questions that complicate the performance model at the local level.

This book is a study of mayoral approval in four cities with long histories of racial conflict: New Orleans, Detroit, Chicago, and Charlotte. Two have white majorities and white mayors; two have black majorities and black mayors; and two are southern cities and two are northern. The cities were chosen for their diverse settings in order to conduct identical studies of the role of performance and race in mayoral approval. The four cities do not represent a larger population in the traditional, scientific sense. The criteria for selecting these cities follows Adam Przeworski and Henry Teune's "most different systems" design, in which the researcher examines models or relationships across a variety of contexts (Przeworski and Teune 2001, 34–39). The theoretical strength of the most different systems design lies in the potential of finding common patterns of behavior across the different systems. In fact, Przeworski and Teune go so far as to say that if the systemic characteristics are differentiated (e.g., white city versus black city), but individual level relationships are similar, "generalizations seem relatively safe" (2001, 42). So, these cities were selected precisely for their differences in order to examine the determinants of mayoral approval.

This first chapter lays the theoretical framework for our test of a performance model of mayoral approval and the role of race in that model. The chapter first reviews the existing research on performance models of presidential and gubernatorial approval. Then follows a discussion of how race can potentially complicate the model at the local level. Here, the term "race" means three things: race as a demographic self-classification; racial attitudes, such as white racism and black consciousness; and racial context, meaning whether the environment is majority black or majority white. All of these racial factors have the potential to affect mayoral approval in racially diverse settings. These factors also have the potential to affect how citizens view the conditions in their cities. Finally, this chapter presents a model of mayoral approval that will be tested in each of the four cities.

Presidential and Gubernatorial Approval

Most of the existing literature on executive approval is based on a performance model that emphasizes citizen evaluations of conditions in the country or state. Thus, performance can be conceived of as the quality of social, economic, and international outcomes experienced by the public (Ostrom and Simon 1985). Performance, then, can theoretically cover an infinite number of subjects, but research has focused on a few factors that seem to be especially crucial in executive approval. The emphasis in this research is on outcomes. Outcomes, not policy proposals or announcements, are crucial influences on executive approval (Brody 1991). For example, the president and his allies take credit for positive outcomes, such as an improved economy or the resolution of a foreign crisis. Since the bulk of this research has been on presidential, as opposed to gubernatorial, approval, we will first review what we know about presidential approval.

Understanding presidential approval requires identifying what it is that the public cares most about. Over time, the focus of the public changes; thus, the basis for evaluating the president also changes. The importance of specific issues to the public changes with objective conditions in the country or the world, such as domestic unrest, terrorism, economic decline, or a foreign crisis. (Edwards et al. 1995). A second general theme in the study of presidential approval is the notion of public expectations. People formulate expectations of a president from campaign promises, policy initiatives, the rhetoric of the opposition, the media, and their own experiences. If these expectations are not met, an "expectations gap" results and presidential approval falls (Waterman et al. 1999). Probably the best illustration of this is the ouster of an incumbent president due to poor economic conditions. Naturally, the newly elected executive would have made economics the cornerstone of his campaign, thus setting up the expectation that times will improve. If that expectation is not realized, the new president's favorable approval rating will not last long.

The third general theme of the performance model is that the public looks back on past performance rather than forward to expected performance. There has been some controversy in performance model research as to whether retrospective or prospective judgments are more important influences on approval ratings and on voting propensities for an incumbent. The original retrospective hypothesis was coined by V. O. Key in his famous statement, "Voters are not fools," meaning that they vote for or against the incumbent based on their perceptions of conditions in the country at the time (Key 1966). More current research also clearly favors the retrospective over the prospective hypothesis. Helmut Norpoth analyzed a series of Gallup poll data on presidential approval and a series of consumer survey data on the economy, spanning the years from 1960 to 1993 (Norpoth 1996). He concluded that, when evaluating the president, citizens ignore forecasts of the future state of the economy. Instead, they evaluate the recent performance of the economy—the retrospective judgment.

Economics is not the only area where retrospective judgments dominate. Arthur H. Miller and Martin P. Wattenberg analyzed the familiar open-ended candidate evaluation questions of the National Election Studies from 1952 to 1980, looking for retrospective versus prospective statements. They examined likes and dislikes for all of the presidential candidates during that time period, not just the incumbent presidents running for reelection. The answers are indicative of how people evaluate political figures. Overall, they found that 67 percent of the open-ended responses could be categorized as retrospective, 29.4 percent could be categorized as prospective, and 3.6 percent could be categorized as mixed (Miller and Wattenberg 1985, 364–65).

Probably the best argument supporting the dominance of retrospective judgments involves the level of sophistication required for prospective judgments. The classic prospective argument regarding economics assumes that voters listen to economic forecasts and judge presidents based on how they expect the economy to perform (MacKuen et al. 1992). Most students of public opinion would be skeptical of any such assumption, given what we know about the general lack of political awareness and information on the part of the public. Yet, the public clearly judges presidents on the basis of domestic and foreign events—judgments which are relatively easy to make and which are more retrospective since the judgment occurs after the event. As Richard Nadeau and his colleagues put it, "interpreting the effects of political variables in terms of reward and punishment seems much more straightforward" (Nadeau et al. 1999, 129).

These general themes of performance evaluations of presidents reveal the substantive topics on which they are judged. First, there is ample evidence that economic evaluations directly affect presidential popularity. In fact, it has almost become conventional wisdom that presidents are rewarded and punished in accordance with fluctuations in the national economy. Both objective and subjective measures of economic performance have been examined as predictors of presidential approval. All of the research has come to the same conclusion: economic factors are a significant part of presidential approval. Furthermore, it appears that economic effects are stronger in recent presidencies than they were in past presidencies (Brody 1991).

What aspects of the economy have the most impact on presidential approval? Research is somewhat mixed on this issue, but among the aggregate economic indicators, inflation and consumer prices appear to be more influential than unemployment (Kernell 1978; MacKuen 1983; Nadeau et al. 1999). This pattern is almost certainly related to the salience of inflation versus unemployment to the electorate as a whole. While unemployment may be a dramatic event to those who experience it, it is not universal. On the other hand, everyone experiences inflation as a decline in real income. For all but the wealthy, inflation involves changes in nearly all aspects of a person's lifestyle. Inflation may not be as dramatic as unemployment, but its cumulative psychic effect can be depressing and long lasting. The effects of inflation on presidential approval are not only stronger than the effects of unemployment; they also persist for a longer period of time (MacKuen 1983).

The other prominent influence on presidential approval is foreign policy, specifically foreign crises. During times of foreign crisis the public's attention is naturally focused on the president—the symbol of the country and the person with the most power over foreign affairs. The role of foreign affairs in presidential approval is so significant that presidents manipulate foreign affairs with high profile summits or tough rhetoric in order to divert attention from domestic problems (Ostrom and Simon 1985).

Since presidential approval was first measured, the effects of foreign policy events have been noticed. The most well-known effect is the "rally" effect, which occurs when there is a positive spike in presidential approval in response to an external threat to the country. Examples of the rally effect would be the Cuban missile crisis, the Gulf of Tonkin Resolution, the 1991 Persian Gulf War, the invasion of Panama, the September 11, 2001 terrorist attack on the United States, and the 2003 invasion of Iraq. During these times, patriotism and anxiety combine to overcome partisanship and produce unusually high levels of presidential support. Due to his position as head of state and government, the president becomes the focal point of public support (Heatherington and Nelson 2003). However, rallies are famous for being short lived (2003, 38). If the foreign crisis is resolved such that the president can claim a positive outcome—as was the case in most of the crises mentioned previously—the public's attention will inevitably return to domestic concerns, and approval eventually will drop. A focus on domestic politics re-activates partisanship, and citizens normally critical of the president will resume their opposition.

If, on the other hand, the crisis is not resolved, or if it is resolved in a manner that is perceived as a "failure" on the part of the United States, then presidential approval will fall even though there may have been an initial rally. The best examples of long-term U.S. foreign crises are the Korean and Vietnam wars. The public eventually viewed both of these wars as ineffective at best and outright failures at worst. The Korean War had a continuing negative influence on Harry Truman's popularity, and Vietnam was a major factor in producing Lyndon B. Johnson's declining approval ratings (Kernell 1978, 519; Hibbs et al. 1982). It is particularly instructive to note that these studies used the number of American casualties in Vietnam and Korea to capture the effects of those wars on presidential approval. There is probably no indicator of foreign-policy failure more powerful than increasing American casualties—at least as far as the public is concerned. In sum, as was the case with the economy, the concept of performance is a determinant of presidential approval.

Any discussion of performance and presidential approval must include the role of the media in priming certain events and issues. The media, by paying more attention to some topics than others, set the agenda by which the public judges the president (Iyengar and Kinder 1987). The impact of an issue or event on presidential approval depends on its salience to the public. For example, if foreign policy is more salient than economics and the president performs well in foreign policy, then his approval ratings will improve, even in a poor economy (Edwards et al. 1995). Media attention is the most important determinant of salience, and the more people are exposed to the media, the more their perceptions of the importance of an issue are affected by that exposure. When public approval of the president increases or decreases, it is not typically because of personal experiences, but rather because of the domestic and foreign policy outcomes reported in the news (Brody 1991; Nadeau et al. 1999). So presidential performance is mediated by the news before it can influence public approval.

Although presidential approval has been studied extensively, researchers know less about why people approve or disapprove of governors. Initially, there was some controversy about the economic performance model in particular and whether it could apply to governors (Chubb 1988; Peltzman 1987). It was originally thought that national, not state, economic conditions impinged upon a governor's popularity, but this approach ignored the likelihood of state differences in economic conditions. States can, and do, vary in economic performance: Some thrive while others languish. Some states are affected more directly by an economic downturn than others. For example, the oil bust of the 1980s affected oil-producing states much more than the remainder of the country, and the decline in manufacturing was particularly hard on the rust belt. Moreover, citizens notice when their state is faring noticeably worse than the nation as a whole (Howell and Vanderleeuw 1990).

Despite the original controversy about whether the economic performance model applies to governors, the bulk of evidence today, both from single-state studies and from national data, indicates that state economic conditions do impact gubernatorial voting and popularity. Most studies of governors examine voting for the incumbent as opposed to incumbent approval, but it is easy to see the relevance of this research to gubernatorial approval. Richard G. Niemi and his colleagues examined thirty-four gubernatorial races by combining ABC/*Washington Post* exit polls for 1986 with data on state economic performance. A state's economic effects on the vote for governor were systematically different depending on whether an incumbent was running or not. Changes in a state's real disposable income had more impact in incumbent races than in nonincumbent races, while perceptions of the national economy had a larger impact in the nonincumbent races. In fact, the national economy was not even significant in the incumbent races (Niemi et al. 1995, 951).

Craig J. Svoboda confirmed this pattern by using a subjective measure of state economies. Instead of using the objective measure—change in disposable income—he used individual evaluations of each state's economy as measured in thirty-five gubernatorial elections in 1984 and 1986 using

CBS/*New York Times* exit polls. Svoboda's argument was that objective conditions may not be accurately reflected in voters' perceptions, but those perceptions were more important in determining vote (Svoboda 1995,146). Using the subjective measure, state economic evaluations were again a key determinant of voter choice in incumbent gubernatorial elections. Open seat contests for governor, in contrast, were more affected by national forces. Thus, the performance model of executive approval operates at the state level as well as at the national level, at least where economics are concerned.

But economic performance is not the only performance measure by which governors can be judged. Theoretically, citizens of a state can hold the governor accountable for educational performance, the condition of state roads, the state's environment, increasing taxes, or corruption in state government, depending on what is most salient to the person. Unfortunately, with the exception of increasing taxes, there is no research examining and comparing the influence that other aspects of state level performance might have on gubernatorial voting or approval. Increasing taxes were negatively related to voting for the incumbent governor in Niemi and colleagues' research, but other state-level dimensions of performance remain unstudied.

Performance Models and Mayors

Public approval is as valuable a resource for mayors as it is for presidents. The circumstances for popularly elected mayors are only different in scope and in the types of issues with which mayors deal. The mayor must be able to convince the city council to support his initiatives, just as the president needs such influence in Congress. The mayor, like the president, must oversee a bureaucracy, many of whom are not his appointees and may not be in agreement with executive orders or policies. Popular approval gives both executives political capital in dealing with these institutions.

The reasoning that underlies the performance model of executive approval can easily be applied to the local level, yet the performance model has rarely been extended to the study of mayors. There are some qualitative differences between the local context and the national and state contexts that, taken together, suggest that a performance model may be even more applicable to mayors than to governors and presidents. First, the concept of performance has a richness and complexity at the local level that is not possible at the two higher levels of government. Citizens can evaluate their cities in terms of the level of crime, the quality of policing, the availability of jobs, recreational opportunities, conditions of streets, public transportation, the schools, and a myriad of other factors affecting the quality of urban life. In contrast, the factors comprising "performance" at the state and national level are likely to be much more limited in scope. In the research cited above, economic conditions are the focal point in the national and state performance models. This is logical since economic indicators such as inflation, changes in real disposable income, and the value of stocks tend to be more uniformly spread across the state or the nation than the factors that comprise local performance. Crime levels vary dramatically from one city to another, as do the availability of jobs, the quality of police forces, recreational opportunities, and the other local performance factors mentioned above. So there is more empirical content at the local level to the concept of performance.

There is also more psychological content to the local level analysis of performance. All of these aspects of urban life can be observed up close in the course of daily life, in contrast to conditions in the state or the nation. Citizens can evaluate the quality of life in their cities firsthand, while citizens obtain most information about state and national conditions from the media. So, in addition to a greater number of factors comprising the concept of local performance, those factors have the potential to be more personal to citizens by virtue of their own experiences.

The national and state level research has drawn a distinction between what has been labeled personal vs. collective judgments about economic conditions. It has been repeatedly shown that voters do not hold the president responsible for their *personal* economic circumstances—the pocketbook voting hypothesis. Instead, the more powerful influence on voting behavior is judgments about conditions in the country as a whole, an impersonal *collective* judgment. Following this reasoning, citizens would not hold a mayor responsible for what they personally experience in their city, only for their assessment of conditions in the city as a whole. However, we argue that the personal vs. collective distinction is blurred at the local level. In cities the collective is where citizens work and live, making it more difficult to separate conditions in the city from conditions in one's own life. For example, if crime is increasing in the urban area where someone lives, it will in all likelihood increase that person's worry about his or her own personal safety. In contrast, if the same person hears about increasing crime in "urban America," the connection to one's personal safety may not be made at all. Again, our point is that performance has a powerful and personal component at the local level.

The performance model's theoretical importance lies in its relation to democratic theory. Ideally, a mayor should be judged by his or her representation of citizens' interests. In an urban setting, survey after survey has shown that citizens name specific quality of life problems when asked what is the biggest problem facing their city (Mohai 1990; Baldassare 2003;

Howell, 1988–2004). The clear message from citizens is that they want positive outcomes, or at least improvements, in areas such as crime, transportation, job availability, and schools. Mayors are the chief executives who oversee the administration of nearly every city service, including the police, and they are increasingly assuming responsibility for the schools as well (Marschall and Shah 2005). Thus, performance, as measured by citizen perceptions of conditions in their cities, is the primary yardstick by which mayors should be evaluated in a democratic society. This is expressed in Hypothesis One:

> Performance is positively and strongly related to mayoral approval.

However, at the local level there is a major complicating factor not present at the state or national level—the presence of African American executives. Over the past twenty years there has been dramatic growth in the number of African American mayors, which introduces race and all of its complications into any test of the performance model and these executives. Actually, most of the existing research on black mayors could be described as following a "racial model" which emphasizes the role of racial identity, racial attitudes, and racial context. In the next sections, we examine the ways in which race might complicate the performance model in explaining approval of both black and white mayors.

Race Confounds the Performance Model

Race, the most basic cleavage in our society, affects many aspects of urban politics in America. Generations of discrimination, current inequalities, and social segregation have produced two cultures which often perceive their interests in conflict. In their classic work *Divided by Color*, Kinder and Sanders (1996) provide a vivid description of the racial divide over a wide variety of attitudes such as party identification, the obligations of the government, welfare, criminal justice and the role of race in American society. At the most fundamental level, blacks and whites disagree on the nature of the racial policy debate. Whites believe that racial discrimination and prejudice are no longer operative, and that blacks need merely work harder, stay out of trouble, and they will have the same opportunities as whites. In other words, whites believe that the playing field is level. Blacks, on the other hand, see discrimination and inequities as pervasive, both in their personal lives and in society as a whole. Kinder and Sanders go so far as to say that "black and white Americans have taken possession of distinct *paradigms*. In the extreme, blacks and whites look upon the social and political world in fundamentally different and mutually unintelligible ways . . . white and black citizens appear to have a terrible time talking to one another about race" (1996, 288). Because of these political and social differences, it is logical that race is front and center in research on urban politics.

In this research we are broadening the concept of race to mean three things. First, and paramount, race is simply self-classification as a member of a particular racial group. This aspect of race is probably the most powerful factor because it is based in a fundamental human need to know who we are in relation to the social world. Social identity theorists assert that humans develop a sense of the social self very early in life, long before other attitudes become meaningful (Dalton 1980). They also contend that social identity is a very powerful psychological construct that not only influences a person's view of oneself, but also affects a person's perceptions of others (Lerner and Miller 1978; Merelman 1986). Thus, it should not be surprising that most research on race focuses on the simple demographic variable.

However, in this research, race or more accurately, racial factors, will be broadened to include attitudes toward racial matters such as white racism and black consciousness, and racial context—the racial composition of the environment. All of these aspects of race have been found to influence political behavior and therefore, deserve a place in models of approval of black and white mayors.

Race as Self-Classification

The increasing number of African American mayors in the United States is made possible primarily by the transformation of many urban areas from majority white to majority black. These transformations are urban social revolutions of a sort, and the repercussions are felt in all segments of urban society: politics, social life, and economics. The word "revolution" is a strong one, but appropriate. The white majority strongly resists the advance of black political power, fearing that it will mean the end of the dominant social and economic position to which they have become accustomed. White reaction most often takes the form of white flight, which solves the problem for those who flee. But for whites who stay, resistance takes the form of using their economic power to isolate themselves and their children in certain neighborhoods and schools, and to bloc vote for white candidates.

Attaining majority status has psychological meaning for blacks that cannot be overestimated. After years of discrimination and exclusion, black citizens in majority black cities believe that they can use the political system to rectify past wrongs and improve their quality of life. They believe that the barriers to their and their children's success can be removed, or at least diminished, with a change in political leadership. These hopes have generally not materialized (Browning, Marshall and Tabb 1990; Reed 1988;

Singh 1998), but that does not prevent blacks from believing that, other things being equal, life will be better for them when blacks are in leadership positions. The most symbolic event in this revolution is the election of a black person to the highest elected position in the city. Thus, it should not be surprising that the election of the first black mayor in any city is cause for much rejoicing in the African American community.

The research on racial polarization that occurs during mayoral elections in racially diverse cities is voluminous and comes to one conclusion—race nearly always affects mayoral elections in these settings, whether the candidates are both white, both black, or one is black and one is white (cf. Giles 1977; Fossett and Kiecolt 1989; Vanderleeuw 1990; Glaser 1994). The tendency to vote within race is both symbolic and instrumental. At the symbolic level, voting for the candidate that shares one's race is based in identification, the perception that this candidate is like the voter, and his or her desire to have a person belonging to his or her "group" in the mayor's office. At the instrumental level, it is well established that blacks and whites often have different policy agendas. Racial differences in public policy preferences at the local level have not been well researched in a systematic fashion. However, from anecdotal evidence it seems that the key racial difference is the white emphasis on economic development and business versus the black emphasis on issues of poverty and crime.

Racial Polarization and the Election of Black Mayors

High levels of racial polarization typically characterize the election of the first black mayor in a city. In these cases there is evidence that some white citizens, who have not voted in the past come to the voting booth for the express purpose of voting against the black candidate (Hahn, Klingman, and Pachon 1976; Browning, Marshall, and Tabb 1990). These "breakthrough" elections are typically the result of years of gradual demographic change whereby blacks become an increasingly larger proportion of the electorate. For blacks, the relative size of the group in the local electorate is critical; larger relative size generates greater electoral mobilization, and mobilization is critical to political incorporation (Browning, Marshall and Tabb 1984). Put simply, blacks win their first mayoral offices by mobilizing black voters.

Over the past three decades there have been numerous examples of high levels of racial polarization in biracial contests involving the election of the first black mayor. A historical overview of the ascendancy of black mayors is provided in Chapter 2. These election stories have strong commonalities, all based on the heightened racial divisions surrounding this historic event, and illustrate how this phenomenon has changed little with time. All of these stories indicate that, thirty years after the 1967 elections of Carl Stokes in Cleveland and Richard Hatcher in Gary, Indiana, and thirty years after the civil rights movement, the election of a first black mayor is still a major racial event. Many voters see in this event implications far beyond a change in the race of the mayor; it is a change in the racial regime.

Possibly the most important illustration of the intractability of racial polarization in racially diverse settings is the role of race in the reelection bids of black incumbent mayors. On the one hand, it is testimony to progress in race relations that incumbent black mayors are typically successful in winning reelection. In an analysis of the outcome of every black incumbent reelection bid in cities larger than 50,000 from 1965 to 1999, 78 percent of black incumbent mayors won reelection (Hajnal 2001). Even more telling, in the majority white cities, where whites could have easily elected a white challenger, the black incumbents won 74 percent of the time against a white opponent, although, we should note that there were only 27 such cases out of 126 elections with black incumbent mayors (2001, 610).

On the other hand, while Hajnal claims that black incumbents tend to receive more white crossover votes in reelections than in the incumbents' initial elections, a closer look at the evidence supporting this conclusion is less convincing. First, while Hajnal claims that the role of race diminishes in the reelections of black mayors, the coefficients for racial threat are essentially the same in the models of first election and reelection (Hajnal 2004, 34). Second, while the average increase in the percent of the white vote received by black mayors from the initial election to the reelection was 6.1 percent, the range of this increase was from -16 percent to +39 percent (2004, 39). Clearly, many of the black incumbents received less white vote in their reelection bids rather than more. In fact, in the twenty-five reelections examined by Hajnal, fifteen black mayors received a larger percentage of the white vote than in their first election and ten received less. Furthermore, several high profile black mayors were among those receiving less white vote in the reelection bid: Harold Washington (Chicago), Ernest Morial (New Orleans), David Dinkins (New York) and Willie Brown (San Francisco). Thus, while there is evidence that, in voting for or against black incumbents, whites do take factors other than race into account, race still remains a substantial consideration.

The mixed evidence on black incumbent reelections illustrates the fundamental question of the performance model of mayoral approval. Are these black mayors evaluated primarily on what they do or don't do to improve conditions in their cities, or does their race overshadow their performance?

Racial Polarization and the Election of White Mayors

While it might be expected that the election of black mayors is characterized by racial polarization, in racially diverse cities it is also often the case that white mayors come to office through racially divisive elections, whether or not they face a black opponent. Recent elections in Ohio, Tennessee, and Florida illustrate the racial nature of elections in cities where blacks constitute at least 20 percent of the population. In 2001 Jane Campbell, a white woman, was elected the first woman mayor of Cleveland. Her opponent was a black former education official under the Clinton administration. In the predominantly white side of town, Campbell won all but 3 of the 167 precincts. Twenty-one black precincts were competitive, but among the 214 remaining black precincts, Campbell won only 17 (Singer 2001). In keeping with racial identification, most voters chose a candidate of their own race.

Voters in Chattanooga also split along racial lines in a biracial mayoral election in 2001. A white businessman defeated eleven other candidates to win the mayoral contest without a runoff by capturing more than two-thirds of the white precincts. The black candidate finished second by receiving more than three-fourths of the votes in the city's predominantly black precincts (Flessner 2001).

The 2003 mayoral race in Orlando, Florida, a city that is 23 percent black, became a racial conflict even though both candidates were white. Early in the campaign, the race card was played when one candidate accused the other of using the "N" word. These accusations came to dominate other issues such as rapid transit and balancing the budget, a strange phenomenon, according to one reporter, since Orlando was not particularly racially tense at the time (Steward 2003). Such is the power of the racial issue once it is activated. While we would expect the Democrat, even without the accusation about racial slurs, to enjoy most of the black and Latino support, what was significant about this election was its strident racial tone. "The race card was played so often, the spots were worn off." (Steward 2003)

In sum, racial polarization is a ubiquitous characteristic of elections in racially diverse cities. The question is not whether racial polarization exists but to what extent.

Implications for Mayoral Approval and the Performance Model

What does the racial history of mayoral elections have to do with mayoral approval? Approval has both conceptual distinctions from voting and commonalities with voting. When a citizen is asked whether or not she approves of a mayor, it is usually asked in terms of an evaluation of performance; voters are asked whether or not they approve of "his handling the job of mayor" or "her performance as mayor." This survey question focuses attention on performance, as opposed to voting, which focuses on choosing between mayoral candidates. In addition, approval confers legitimacy beyond the election and has the potential to affect the mayor's ability to govern. What voting and approval have in common is a basic evaluative component; both are forms of expressing positive or negative assessments of the mayor or the candidate.

The evidence of the effects of race on elections is overwhelming, so it would be surprising if the same pattern did not hold for approval. Like elections, approval will reflect existing cleavages in the city. The election results from these settings indicate that there are some white voters who would never vote for a black mayoral candidate in a biracial election. These whites are also unlikely to approve of the black mayor's performance regardless of what he or she actually accomplishes. Likewise, there are black voters who would never vote for the white candidate over a black candidate, and as a consequence will never approve of the elected white mayor. These types of voters represent the extremes of racial animosity, but the election results indicate that many urban citizens simply view politics in their city through a racial lens.

For citizens to view politics in their city from a racial perspective has serious implications for the performance model. Many of the mayor's actions and policies, regardless of their genesis or rationale, will be interpreted by many as favoring one race or the other. If he or she emphasizes economic development it will be seen as insensitive to low income people, who are often blacks. If the mayor emphasizes improving the quality of life for the poor, or the empowerment of the poor, it will often be interpreted as unfavorable to business, since such policies usually require some redistribution of wealth. Mayors in racially diverse cities walk a tightrope between two groups who believe their interests are at odds.

This is not to say that performance does not influence mayoral approval. Recall that Hypothesis One is that performance is positively and strongly related to the approval of both white and black mayors. What is at issue is the magnitude of the additional direct effect that race has in explaining mayoral approval in racially diverse cities.

Descriptive and Substantive Representation

The relative impact of race and performance in predicting approval of the mayor is another way of approaching the question of descriptive versus substantive representation. Descriptive representation (sometimes called symbolic representation) means that constituents are represented by officials who resemble them demographically; the officials reflect the citizens on variables such as race, gender, religion, ethnicity, et cetera. Descriptive representation has value in that it indicates that members of a group, such as blacks, are not totally excluded from positions of power, and it provides role models for other members of the group (Canon 1999). Descriptive representation can be politically empowering. Blacks in cities with black mayors are more participatory, trusting, and politically knowledgeable than blacks in cities without black mayors (Bobo and Gilliam, Jr. 1990). In addition to these political effects, there is the argument that a black presence among elected officials reduces the overt expression of racism (Thernstrom 1987).

However, in her comprehensive study of the effects on blacks of having a black representative in the U.S. Congress, Katharine Tate, found that descriptive representation in Congress was not politically empowering. Blacks represented by blacks were no more interested in political campaigns, efficacious, or likely to vote than blacks represented by nonblacks. She suggests that the reason her findings differ from those of Lawrence Bobo and Franklin Gilliam, Jr. is that the impact of black officeholders is more apparent at the local level, especially when a black mayor is involved (Tate 2003, 141). The distinction implies that black citizens are more likely to connect and identify with a black mayor than with a black congressperson or other national or state figure, which makes sense given that the mayor is closer to home, both physically and in terms of the issues he deals with.

In our mayoral approval research, the psychic value of descriptive representation is indicated by the effects of race on mayoral approval while controlling for perceptions of performance. To the extent that urban citizens evaluate the mayor on the basis of a racial match with themselves, they are conveying that they value descriptive representation.

Substantive representation is quite different. Substantive representation means that concrete interests and needs of a group are being advanced. In the case of blacks it means representation that affects public policies of interest to blacks or improvements in their quality of life. Does having black elected officials make a tangible difference for black citizens? Whether studying black mayors or black U.S. Representatives, the same conclusion is reached: "black officials have not been successful in solving the intractable problems of the black underclass" (Perry 1996, 6; see also Browning, Marshall and Tabb 1990; Singh 1998).

If we shift our focus from the daunting task of addressing poverty to benefits in other areas, there is evidence of substantive representation. Black incumbents in city government can make incremental changes in local hiring policies and spending priorities (Eisinger 1982; Mladenka 1989), and black representatives on school boards affect the direction of educational policy (Meier and England 1984). Probably the most optimistic substantive effects of black representation have been found in a study by David Canon of the black members of the U.S. House of Representatives. Canon thoroughly rejects the "no racial effects" model, finding that black members of the House are more attentive to the needs of their black constituents than are the white representatives who have substantial numbers of black constituents. In Canon's research, substantive representation of blacks is measured by roll call voting, sponsoring legislation, speeches, the content of constituency newsletters, racial composition of the staff, the placement of district offices, and other behaviors that are part and parcel of the job of a U.S. Representative. While these indicators of substantive representation are certainly of value, they do not measure any direct effects on black citizens.

In this research, substantive representation is measured closer to home. My interpretation of substantive representation is positive citizen evaluations of local government performance. All urban citizens, black and white, are "substantively represented" when they are satisfied with the quality of life and government services in their city. They are not substantively represented when they negatively evaluate the performance of local government on issues such as crime, the police, streets, local job opportunities, parks, schools, and other aspects of urban life. To the extent that urban citizens attach importance to this form of substantive representation, it is expected to affect their approval of the mayor.

Racial Context and the Performance Model

While it might seem that the relationship of race to mayoral approval is fairly straightforward, that is, blacks like the black mayor more than whites do, our actual hypothesis is that this simple relationship is conditioned by a powerful factor—racial context.

Researchers are increasingly realizing that models of political behavior developed in one setting cannot necessarily be generalized to other settings. Social science relationships are context-sensitive, and we must either model context explicitly or acknowledge the limitations of our studies. Context can mean virtually anything relevant about the research setting, such as the level of poverty or economic development, the nature of media messages or the amount of interparty competition. In his seminal essay "The New Look in Public Opinion Research," Paul Sniderman argues that considering context acknowledges the "dynamics of politics"—the theory that results are often variable across contexts (1993, 234).

The aspect of context of interest in this research is the racial composition of the city. Besides race as a demographic, racial context has the most potential to affect the operation of the performance model of mayoral approval. The simple question of whether the city is majority white or majority black permeates all research questions concerning performance and mayoral approval in settings of black/white diversity. Racial context is expected to be influential because it compares the "normal" social order, whites in the majority, to a reverse of that normal social order when blacks are in the majority.

Social dominance theory tells us that societies are organized around the notion of dominant and subordinate groups, with the dominant groups possessing a disproportionate amount of wealth, power, status, et cetera. The dominant group will naturally seek to maintain its dominance through instrumental means such as formal laws or informal discrimination, and through psychological means, such as the perpetuation of values and beliefs that support their dominant position (Sidanius 1993; Sidanius and Pratto 1999; Sidanius et al. 2000). Thus, the majority black city with a black mayor represents a violation of expected group positions because blacks hold not only the top executive office, but probably most of the important public sector offices as well.

This "trading places" phenomenon has great significance to both the previously subordinate group and the previously dominant group. For the previously subordinate group it means that they have some hope of access to the privileges and material goods of the previously dominant group. For the previously dominant group it means anxiety about losing their privileged status and its benefits. For both, the change is a major alteration of their political environment.

A more specific theoretical variation of social dominance theory, the group competition model devised by Bobo, is also relevant to our performance model of mayoral approval in racially diverse settings (Bobo 1988a, 1988b, 2000; Bobo and Hutchings 1996). The group competition model focuses on the extent to which group members feel that their group is threatened with the loss of resources to other groups. This model presumes that citizens perceive competition between groups as a zero-sum game in which their losses are another group's gains. This model does not predict that all groups feel the same level of competition with other groups; those with more resources naturally feel less competition, and those with fewer resources feel more competition (Bobo and Hutchings 1996, 958).

This model is particularly applicable to urban settings where competition for resources is very real, tangible, and close to home. It is quite realistic for groups to see themselves in competition with other groups for jobs, public offices, quality schools, and neighborhoods. According to Bobo and Vincent Hutchings, this competition is exacerbated between blacks and whites because blacks feel high levels of group competition due to their subordinate position in society, and among whites, the feeling of group competition is partly based in antiblack animosity.

Racial context affects both blacks and whites. Among whites, racial context has been shown to affect animosity toward blacks, racial policy attitudes and party registration. Using the southern white respondents in four American National Election Studies, James Glaser (1994) added the percent of blacks in the survey respondents' county to the data and found that this measure of the racial environment had a large impact on their attitudes toward black political and social progress. Specifically, whites in heavily black areas were most hostile to black political aspirations and to black political power.

Racial environment can even affect the political party membership of whites. In a study of Republican party registration in Louisiana between 1976 and 1990, Michael Giles and Kaenan Hertz (1994) found that as the percentage that blacks constituted of the voting age population grew larger, there was a larger increase in the percentage of whites registering as Republican.

Marylee Taylor conducted the two most comprehensive studies of the effects of racial context on whites. For her 1998 and 2000 studies, she utilized national data from the 1990 and 1994 General Social Surveys. The results were quite clear. The percent black in the local population was positively associated with three types of antiblack racial attitudes: traditional prejudice, opposition to race-targeted programs, and the belief that blacks have advantages over whites. Taylor goes so far as to say that researchers can use the "local racial proportion effects to detect the influence of racial sentiment on policy opinions and related beliefs" (2000, 134).

Perhaps the most striking example of the effects of racial composition are those found in the 1990 Louisiana U.S. Senate race involving David Duke, arguably the most visible racist candidate in recent American history. Despite a variety of control variables, support for Duke was positively related to the percent black in the local context (Giles and Buckner 1993). All of these findings are quite consistent with the group competition model. Among whites, resistance to racial change is a response to the possibility of losing something to blacks.

The racial environment also affects blacks, but in different ways. The contextual factor utilized in these studies is not the percent black in a geographic area, but the presence or absence of a black mayor. Thus, the contextual factor is actual political empowerment, not the potential for political empowerment. The most comprehensive study of empowerment effects on blacks was conducted by Bobo and Gilliam (1990) who examined the largest cities in the primary sampling units of the 1987 General Social Survey. Having a black mayor was associated with a number of positive civic traits among blacks, such as trust in local government, efficacy, political information, and political participation (see also Emig, Hesse and Fisher 1996; Gilliam and Kaufman 1998). Empowerment clearly gives a psychic boost to blacks, which is exactly what the group competition model predicts will happen when an outgroup gains access to political power. Furthermore, the boost in efficacy and participation is more evident among blacks with less education and income—those who were most disadvantaged under the previous system (Gallup-Black 2003).

It follows from the theories and empirical findings cited above that the racial composition of the city will affect the workings of the traditional performance model of executive approval. We expect its effects to be felt primarily through interactions with other variables, that is, we hypothesize relationships to be different in white cities as compared to black cities. The full scope of these interactions will be explored later in this chapter. For now consider the relationship between race and mayoral approval. Social dominance theory would predict that a black mayor elected in a majority black city would bring greater attention to racial matters simply by being an exception to the norm of white executives. Thus, Hypothesis Two is that:

> Race will have direct and independent effects on mayoral approval, regardless of evaluations of performance evaluations, and these effects are expected to be greater in the case of black mayors.

Race and Performance Evaluations

Race can also affect mayoral approval indirectly by influencing citizens' judgments of performance. That is, race may be antecedent to the performance model and affect citizens' perceptions of conditions in the city. If this is so, omission of the influence of race on perceptions of performance would provide an incomplete description of how the performance model works. Since it is well established that, due to different life experiences, group interests, and socialization, blacks and whites have different perceptions across a variety of domains, they may also have differing evaluations of local government services, crime, employments prospects, and other conditions.

Research on citizen satisfaction with urban services does demonstrate racial polarization in citizen satisfaction with urban services, with blacks having more negative perceptions (Van Ryzin et al. 2004; McGuire Research Services 2000, 2001; Muzzio and Van Ryzin 2000, 2001; Ohio State University Center for Survey Research 2002). The question is not whether racial differences in performance evaluations exist, but, rather, what is the explanation for those differences. On the one hand, racial differences can be based in the difference of social service delivery in middle class, predominantly white neighborhoods compared to low income, predominantly black neighborhoods. Because middle class homeowners carry more clout with city hall due to their economic power, they may receive a higher quality of service from local government. This explanation means that there is a link between objective conditions and citizen perceptions of those conditions.

Another explanation for the racial gap in performance evaluations is more psychological, less objective, and based in the group competition and social dominance theories mentioned earlier. Because whites and blacks occupy the extreme positions of privilege and underprivilege in American society, it is only reasonable that they would view some aspects of their environment differently. Specifically, the disadvantaged group would be expected to hold more negative views regardless of their personal economic status or the conditions of their specific neighborhood.

Research indicates that both objective neighborhood conditions and individual characteristics such as race and income influence how urban residents perceive conditions in their cities. A study conducted in St. Louis found that more police officers on patrol in a neighborhood produced more positive evaluations of the police (Parks 1984). On the other hand, Karin Brown and Philip Coulter (1983) found no link between the quality of the services provided and citizen perceptions of those services, leading them to suggest that citizen perceptions might be affected by race, income, or other individual characteristics. Twenty years later, using data from the Survey of Satisfaction with New York City Services, 2000, Gregg Van Ryzin and his colleagues concluded that both neighborhood conditions and race influence citizen satisfaction with services (Van Ryzin et al. 2004). Despite different findings, all of these scholars and others agree that the quality of urban services varies by neighborhood, and when attempting to explain why people are positive or negative about a particular city service, we must include neighborhood variables along with individual characteristics in the models.

The research detailed in this book is about the individual characteristic, race, not about varying objective conditions in low versus middle income neighborhoods, nor about individual socioeconomic status, although all of these are certainly related. Race, in this research, represents a view of the world from the standpoint of advantage and status versus disadvantage and a lack of status, regardless of an individual's income or education or the conditions in their neighborhood. So we must find a way to separate the more global group-based differences from objective conditions in neighborhoods and individual socioeconomic status when we attempt to explain citizen perceptions of conditions in their cities.

The expectation that blacks will have more negative views than whites of local government performance is hypothesized to be particularly apparent in majority white contexts. In majority white cities, the typical balance of power relationship exists, with whites in control both economically and politically. Under these circumstances, the group competition model and social dominance theory both suggest that blacks, as the subordinate group, will have more negative views of local conditions. But what if blacks are in the majority, and hold political, if not economic, power?

Before jumping to the conclusion that blacks will have more positive views than whites of conditions in a majority black city, we must first take into account the objective conditions that plague most majority black cities. It is a familiar story. Dwindling jobs, poor schools, crime, and deteriorating housing are just a few examples of the multitude of challenges facing black mayors in majority black cities (Barnes 1994; Nelson 1990; Preston 1990; Kraus and Swanstrom 2001). As a consequence of this objective reality we expect both white and black evaluations of performance to be lower in the majority black cities than in majority white cities. However, for blacks, the psychological boost of political power may mitigate the negative effect of their conditions (Marschall 2005; Marschall and Ruhil 2005), resulting in only slightly lower evaluations of conditions. On the other hand, for whites who live in majority black contexts, both the objective and the psychological factors work in the same direction. The poor conditions will be met with a very negative response among whites because of their need to adopt beliefs and attitudes that support their dominant position in society (Sidanius et al. 2000). Blaming the black majority, which is also the outgroup, gives justification for negative perceptions of conditions in the majority black city. If these countervailing forces are accurate, white and black performance evaluations will be more similar, and lower, in majority black cities than in majority white cities. Thus, Hypothesis Three is that:

> Blacks are more negative than whites about evaluations of performance, and the difference is accentuated in majority white cities.

Racial Attitudes and the Performance Model

The third way in which race influences the performance model is through the influence of racial attitudes on both the evaluations of performance and on mayoral approval. Since the crucial racial attitudes are different for whites and blacks, we are now referring to intraracial differences as opposed to black/white differences. First, let us consider the racial attitudes of whites.

White Racial Attitudes

White racial attitudes have been an integral part of the partisan and ideological continuum since 1964 (Carmines and Stimson 1989; Edsall and Edsall 1992), and volumes have been written on their impact on elections and public policy opinions. Whites' racial attitudes are not only a component of partisanship and ideology, but also part and parcel of other values such as beliefs about the role of government and egalitarianism. Furthermore, specific issues such as welfare, poverty programs, and ways to prevent crime are highly colored by racial attitudes among whites.

White racial attitudes also influence presidential elections. The effects of racial attitudes on white voting in presidential elections are, at minimum, felt indirectly through their impact on other values and predispositions such as ideology, candidate evaluations, and party identification. These values and predispositions, in turn, exercise direct effects on voting in presidential elections. However, in certain elections, one of the presidential candidates will emphasize racial stereotypes or racial policies, and in these cases white racial attitudes can exert direct effects on vote. In these types of elections the direct influence of racial attitudes adds to the already existing indirect effects through the other predispositions.

Empirical evidence for direct effects of racial attitudes in presidential elections comes most recently from the 1988 election. In 1988, Jesse Jackson ran respectably in several Democratic presidential primaries as the first major black presidential candidate in American history. His candidacy naturally activated racial predispositions among both whites and blacks. Among whites, support for George H. W. Bush rose steadily with increases in antiblack attitudes—what Kinder and Sanders label "racial resentment" (1996, 245). Furthermore, the effect of these antiblack attitudes was greatest among Independents who had no anchoring partisanship. The infamous Willie Horton ad[1] further activated racial attitudes in the 1988 presidential election. As whites became more exposed to the ad and the surrounding controversy, their racial attitudes became more closely tied to their votes (1996, 247). Kinder and Sanders conclude that, "race was in fact central to the 1988 contest" (1996, 252).

In their analysis of individual voting decisions in the 1992 presidential election, Warren Miller and Merrill Shanks detected only indirect effects of white racial attitudes, probably because race was less apparent in the conduct of the 1992 campaign itself. These authors conclude that any impact of racial attitudes on voting should be attributed to their impact through other partisan or policy-related dispositions, such as beliefs about equality (1996, 312–13). Miller and Shanks shy away from concluding that white voters' attitudes toward race-related topics are causally prior to these other

[1] The Willie Horton ad portrayed a black man who had been released by a trustee program and subsequently murdered a woman. The photo of the black man was perceived as very threatening. This ad was run by the 1988 Bush campaign to portray Democrats as weak on crime, with the side effect of reinforcing racial stereotypes.

dispositions, but their own evidence, along with the impact that white racial attitudes have had in altering partisan cleavages, suggest otherwise.

Our settings of racially diverse cities present a situation where the effects of white racial attitudes should be more pronounced than in the nation as a whole. Because blacks comprise only 11 percent of the U.S. population, for most whites, racial issues are largely symbolic and not consequential for their everyday lives. In racially diverse cities, the local media and citizens' personal experiences prime whites' racial attitudes daily, whether liberal or conservative, activating both symbolic and instrumental racial considerations. In fact, it is nearly impossible for a person to avoid thinking about his or her racial views in racially diverse areas, whether he or she is in the minority or the majority. Yet, in spite of the racial competition in these settings, there has been very little empirical research on the impact of whites' racial views on their local political behavior or their attitudes toward local officials.

The most extensive systematic research on the impact of white racial attitudes on local political behavior has focused on elections involving Tom Bradley, a candidate for both mayor of Los Angeles and governor of California. From 1969 to 1982, various measures of white racism affected white voting behavior in elections involving Tom Bradley, regardless of the opponent (Citrin et al. 1990; Sears and Kinder 1971; Kinder and Sears 1981). Most notably, in the Los Angeles mayoral elections between Bradley and Sam Yorty, racial attitudes were shown to be major determinants of voting behavior even when controlling for other political attitudes.

Other evidence of the influence of whites' racial attitudes comes from experimental studies in which the race of a hypothetical candidate is varied as the experimental treatment. Experimental designs are superior for the study of race because they remove the complications of actual candidates, disguise the racial focus of the study, and vary only the trait of interest—race—thereby providing firmer evidence of causality. Experiments in Detroit, Los Angeles, and Kentucky all conclude that white racial attitudes impact evaluations of black candidates (Reeves 1997; Terkildsen 1993; McDermott 1998).

On the other hand, the evidence from yet another city is to the contrary. In models of approval of the black mayor of New Orleans, Susan Howell and William McLean (2001) did not find significant effects of white racial attitudes in either of two surveys they utilized, in spite of the fact that both approval of this mayor and voting for this mayor were strongly related to the race of respondents. Thus, while the research is not unanimous, and is geographically limited, the weight of the evidence points to a role for white racial attitudes in a performance model of mayoral approval.

Our hypothesis regarding the impact of white racial attitudes is based on the prominence of race as the critical political and economic cleavage in racially diverse cities. Racial attitudes are simply another manifestation of that cleavage. White urban residents vary in the extent to which they hold antiblack attitudes, and these attitudes are expected to impinge on approval of both white and black mayors. Thus, Hypothesis Four is that:

> Conservative white racial attitudes are positively related to approval of white mayors and negatively related to approval of black mayors.

White racial attitudes can also affect mayoral approval indirectly through evaluations of performance. When the expected social order is reversed, as in majority black cities, anxieties and hostility within the previously dominant group will naturally be activated. There is no reason to assume that the hostility will be directed only toward public officials of the new majority. The new white minority may also fear and anticipate general decline in the city as a whole. This, of course, is the basis for white flight. But, for white citizens who stay, given their loss of status and political power, it is reasonable to expect them to perceive that conditions in the city are changing for the worse. And given that objective conditions often do deteriorate in majority black cities, the perceptions and predictions of the new white minority are reinforced.

Moreover, even without knowledge of or experience with a particular city service or condition, the newly displaced white citizens with the most antiblack attitudes may conclude that city services are worsening simply because blacks are in political control. Psychologists call this the "transfer of affect"—the tendency for positive and negative feelings about one object, in this case the black administration, to be generalized to related objects (Lorge and Curtiss 1936; Osgood and Tannenbaum 1955). This same phenomenon occurs at the national level when we observe that Republicans are more likely to say the economy is improving when there is a Republican president. Thus, Hypothesis Five is:

> In a majority black context, conservative white racial attitudes are negatively related to evaluations of performance. A reverse relationship is expected in majority white contexts.

Black Racial Attitudes

We also expect black citizens' racial attitudes to affect the way blacks view both the mayor and evaluations of performance in these racially diverse cities. However, the relevant racial attitudes for blacks are quite different from the relevant racial attitudes for whites. The most crucial black racial attitude is some form of black consciousness or racial identity, an awareness that being black has special meaning and that blacks have common interests. This concept, like white racial attitudes, has several dimensions. One of the most prominent is Michael Dawson's notion of "linked fate," the belief that one's own life chances are linked to those of blacks as a group (Dawson 1994). According to Dawson, because of widespread historic discrimination against blacks, it is much more efficient for blacks to determine what is good for them individually by determining what is good for blacks as a racial group. That is, whatever is perceived to be good for the group is a psychological shortcut to knowing what is good for an individual. This is efficient because looking to the group is an easy way to determine whether a mayor, a public policy, or anything else, is in someone's interest, and it works because a variety of information sources in the black community reinforce the salience of their racial group interests.

A related form of black consciousness is black solidarity or black autonomy, the notion that blacks need to join together in social, educational, and political endeavors in order to protect their interests. The difference between black solidarity and linked fate is that black solidarity represents an explicit political activism, while linked fate is a more general social group identity (Gurin et al. 1989). Black solidarity, measured in a variety of ways, inclines blacks to work to develop the black community and to belong to organizations to benefit blacks (Bledsoe et al. 1995). Blacks with higher levels of solidarity are also more likely to participate in politics (Olsen 1970; Verba and Nie 1972; Shingles 1981). The aspect of black solidarity that is most relevant for our research on mayoral approval is its link with evaluations of black officials (Gurin et al. 1989).

While a large majority of blacks have some sense of linked fate (Sniderman and Piazza 2002), the degree of that linkage varies among individuals. Similarly, the belief that blacks need to work together for the advancement of their race is not held with equal intensity by all blacks. These variations within the black community have predictable implications for the performance model. High levels of black consciousness, whether linked fate or black solidarity, should be associated with pride in having a black mayor and therefore a greater tendency to approve of him or her. Similarly, high levels of black consciousness should be associated with more positive evaluations of conditions in the majority black city due to the "psychic boost" of living in one of the few settings of black empowerment in America. The opposite is expected to occur in white cities with white mayors; blacks with high levels of racial consciousness should be less approving of the white mayor and less positive about conditions in the city than blacks with low levels of racial consciousness. There is evidence of this "white environment" effect at the national level in Michael Dawson's study of the blacks surveyed by the 1984 and 1988 National Black Election Studies, in which black evaluations of the national economy were affected by their racial group interests (Dawson 1994 85, 86). These expectations are expressed in our final two hypotheses, which are parallel to the hypotheses regarding white racial attitudes. Hypothesis Six is that:

> Black consciousness, whether linked fate or black solidarity, is positively related to approval of black mayors and negatively related to approval of white mayors.

Hypothesis Seven stipulates that:

> In a majority black context, black consciousness is positively related to evaluations of performance. A reverse relationship is expected in majority white contexts.

We have graphically summarized all of the hypotheses above in Figure 1.1.

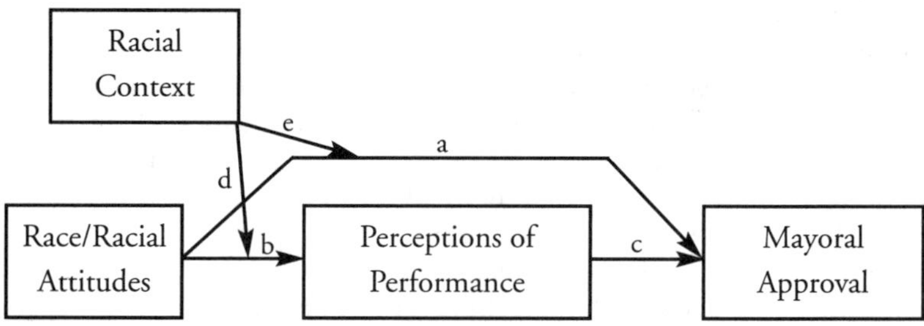

Figure 1.1

Path c represents the original performance model, that perceptions of conditions in the city directly affect approval of the mayor. All other paths represent the potential confounding effects of race on the original performance model. Race and racial attitudes are expected to influence mayoral approval both directly (path a) and indirectly through perceptions of performance (path b). Racial context, defined as whether the city is majority white or majority black, is an overarching factor which alters the nature of the effects of race and racial attitudes (paths d and e). In the next chapters we will test this model by testing all seven hypotheses in four racially diverse cities and, hopefully, shed light on how performance and race each contribute to why citizens like or dislike their mayor.

Chapter 2

Black Mayors in America: A Historical Overview

Chapter Written by Ronald H. Bayor

The election of black mayors in majority white, majority black or multi-racial cities has been difficult and has generally added to the racial tensions in the city. Maynard Jackson, Atlanta's first black mayor commented, "As the first black mayor, I had to deal with exaggerated white anxiety and . . . exaggerated black expectations" (Bayor 1996, 48). This has been the situation in many cities as racial barriers in politics have been torn down.

Black political empowerment through mayoral elections came at a time of urban race riots and white flight during the 1960s. Richard Hatcher of Gary, Indiana and Carl Stokes of Cleveland, Ohio were both elected in 1967. The 1960s were a tumultuous time for America, and its cities indicated the explosiveness of that decade. The assassinations of Malcolm X in 1965 and Martin Luther King, Jr. in 1968 along with the frustrations associated with long-term poverty, police brutality, unemployment, inadequate schools, and white intransigence led to the turmoil visible on the streets in many American cities.

Black mayors often inherited economically and racially troubled cities. Even in cities where the majority of white residents were willing to support black candidates, it was often within the context of race-based outbreaks of violence. In a number of cases, whites thought that a black mayor could calm the tensions. Even in majority black cities, where relatively few white votes were needed for the election of a black mayor, white fears played a major role during the campaign and especially during the governing years. Nonetheless, the racial shift was occurring. In 1991, "thirty cities with populations of fifty thousand or more," had African American mayors and among those, sixteen cities were majority white (Colburn 2001, 24).

This chapter surveys selected U.S. cities that elected black mayors and offers an analysis of the racial situation in each. Richard Hatcher's 1967 victory in Gary, Indiana was the result of 96 percent of the black vote and 12 percent of the white vote—mostly liberal and Jewish—supporting him. The city had a 39 percent black population in 1960 which had grown to 53 percent by 1970 (Keiser 1997). Gary was a typical rustbelt city facing deindustrialization, white flight, increasing black in-migration and increased stress on social services as the tax base eroded. It was difficult to govern even with an infusion of Great Society money. Although Hatcher was reelected a number of times in Gary, he faced the usual problems that often face black mayors of not being able to turn his mayoral political power into economic power for the city's black population, and dealing with a white economic elite that was not interested in the plight of low-income blacks and their declining neighborhoods. According to one politico in Gary, Hatcher's focus was "civil rights, civil rights, and civil rights"(Lane 2001, 71). However, the attention he paid to systemic inequities won him a great deal of support from his constituents. Focusing on ghetto neighborhoods and trying to uplift the poorer residents in Gary, Hatcher helped the city avoid race riots and presided at a time when Gary blacks had "the highest proportions of [black] homeownership in the nation" (Lane 2001, 72). He was also able to place more blacks in important government positions (Keiser 1997).

Although far removed from the rustbelt economy and deindustrialization, Atlanta's Maynard Jackson faced similar race-related problems during his first term. Jackson was elected vice mayor in 1969 in the first election that broke the hold of the white business elite on city hall. By 1973 black registered voters were 49 percent of the total voting population, but this would be the last time whites held the voting majority. Racial rhetoric marked this campaign as the incumbent mayor and Jackson's opponent, Sam Massell proclaimed that "Atlanta's too young to die" and accused Jackson of never favoring anything "that wasn't initiated by a racial viewpoint" (*Atlanta Constitution* 1973), indicating that a black mayor would destroy the city. Massell, a white mayor who had done much for the black community in his one term, resorted to these tactics in a panicked attempt to save his career. Others picked up his strategy. One of Atlanta's neighborhood newspapers, *Northside News*, claimed that Atlanta would follow the same downward trend as other cities with black mayors such as Newark (Bayor 1996). Jackson won the runoff election by taking 95 percent of the black vote and 17 percent of the white vote (Bayor 1996).

However, the new mayor of Atlanta found he had to work with an inhospitable white business elite. Jackson's attempt to bring blacks into an equal partnership in the city's power structure led to charges that he was anti-white. Downtown businesses threatened to leave the city. The mayor's assertion of power brought out the racial tensions that had been generally kept under the surface in this image-conscious city. Whites held firm to their image of Atlanta as "a city too busy to hate." In reality, Atlanta had always been the opposite. Former mayor Ivan Allen, Jr. answered the business community's threat to leave the downtown area. Speaking before a meeting of the business leaders and the mayor, Allen said, "Some of us have gotten too concerned with wanting the city government to fail because it's black" (Bayor 2001, 50). He called for racial harmony. Allen understood white motivations as did black leaders who felt that "there was a Vietnam-type burn-and-reclaim strategy. Let the city go to hell, blame it on the blacks, and they [whites] will come back and rebuild, come back to reclaim it" (Bayor 1996, 50). Jackson actually had to proclaim that "black people do not want to take over Atlanta. Black people want to participate and to have our influence felt in fair proportions" (Bayor 1996, 50). It was the overturning of the usual way of doing business that upset the whites.

The Atlanta situation reveals the basic disconnect between what whites and blacks wanted. As Ivan Allen noted, the problem was that each racial group had a different definition of racial harmony. The "white community tends to define that as absence of disturbance, [the] Negro Community as establishment of their full rights as American citizens" (Bayor 1996, 41*)*. Jackson, like other black mayors, was therefore in a position that made racial tensions evident. Some mayors were able to push through their programs of affirmative action and power sharing regardless, but others, such as Jackson, as will be discussed later, were eventually co-opted by white economic leaders as their first terms ended and they looked toward reelection. Even in majority black cities, such as Gary and Atlanta, African American mayors realized that their success was tied to "the attitude and commitment of local business leaders and whether they were looking to invest in the city" (Lane 2001, 74).

Majority white cities, such as Cleveland, that elected black mayors faced similar issues. Carl Stokes, elected in 1967, in a city with only a 37 percent black population had to run a campaign that de-emphasized race. As he said during his first bid for this office in 1965, "I want to get the Negro question out of the way, then we can talk about issues. My election would not mean a Negro takeover; it would not mean the establishment of a Negro cabinet. My election would mean that the mayor just happened to come from the Negro group" (Moore 2001, 83). Stokes needed to win a higher percentage of whites than Hatcher or Jackson to secure a victory. Playing on white fears after a race riot in 1966, Stokes convinced the business community that he would be able to avoid further racial conflict. He campaigned heavily in white neighborhoods, but met resistance in Cleveland's white ethnic enclaves. Much like Atlanta's white and black mayors, Stokes noted that racial violence was not good for business. Although capturing only 15 percent of the white vote in the December primary, Stokes had enough votes to win after a strong victory in black areas. The general election saw Stokes winning 95 percent of the black vote and 19.3 percent of the white vote, thereby securing enough white business and middle-class voters to be elected mayor (Moore 2001; Nelson and Meranto 1977).

Stokes was successful on a number of levels in regard to the city's racial issues. Securing a restoration of federal urban renewal money and maintaining racial peace in Cleveland after the assassination of Martin Luther King, Jr. won him more support from the white business community. Desirous of keeping the peace, the white business leaders threw their support to Stokes's "Cleveland Now!" plan which would provide funds to deal with such factors as housing, jobs, and health. However, his first term was also filled with some racial violence, problems with police brutality, and a cheating scandal in the police department (Moore 2001).

Another example of a black mayor elected in a majority white city is Philadelphia's Wilson Goode. Goode ran against former mayor Frank Rizzo, who had used racially divisive issues in a previous campaign. In 1983, however, Rizzo and Goode de-emphasized race, each for their own reasons. Rizzo was trying to secure some black votes in this city where blacks were 39 percent of the registered voters and not upset the white reformist segment that was racially liberal. Goode needed to show that he would be mayor of all Philadelphians and did not want to alienate whites with a campaign aimed at blacks. Instead he stressed economic growth (Keiser 1997). During the campaign he surprised voters of both races by recruiting two hundred citizens to help choose the top aides for his administration—he then actually followed their advice in selecting his top administrators (Munoz and Henry 1986).

The election, however, showed racial polarization even if the campaign did not focus on race. Goode took 97 percent of the black vote and 23 percent of the white vote, and was particularly strong among white liberals. In his reelection campaign in 1987, Goode received a similar vote with 97 percent of the black and 18 percent of the white vote (Keiser 1997).

Black mayors of majority white cities particularly walked a tightrope of trying to please both their white and black constituents. Reelection campaigns brought all the issues to the fore. But whether majority white or black, securing enough white voters and pleasing the white business elite were always problems.

In some cities, other minority groups became important players. New York City is a good example of the role of groups such as Latinos as well as the ever-present role of white business leaders. David Dinkins became the first black mayor of New York in 1990 by stressing the issue of racial rapprochement. At this time, New York was 43.2 percent white, 25.2 percent black, and 14.3 percent Latino. Ed Koch was the city's incumbent mayor and Dinkins's opponent in the 1989 Democratic primary. Koch had presided over a city torn by racial incidents. His administration favored New York's whites in a number of racially tense situations. The primary gave Dinkins victory with 84.8 percent of black votes, 60.4 percent of Latino votes, and about 33 percent of white votes. The one-third of whites who supported Dinkins indicates the city's liberal bloc, anti-Koch attitudes, and desire for racial peace. Koch had largely ignored and antagonized the blacks and Latinos. Racial polarization was more evident in the general election when Dinkins defeated the Republican Rudolph Giuliani. Dinkins took 89 percent of the black vote, 73.6 percent of the Latino vote, but only about 25 percent of the white vote. Thus, in spite of the Democratic Party's strong endorsement of Dinkins candidacy, less than half of the white Democrats supported him (Biles 2001; WABC TV/*New York Daily News* Exit Poll 1989). Moreover, the traditional white Democratic vote did not go to Dinkins. He lost white moderates' support and only marginally secured a majority of white liberals. Even the Jewish community, which tended to be liberal and Democratic, supported Giuliani by 65 percent to 35 percent (WABC TV/*New York Daily News* Exit Poll 1989).

As mayor of a multiracial city, Dinkins had the usual problems of keeping his supporters, but in this case his supporters were more than black voters. He also had to reach out to Latinos and others. Each of these groups looked to the mayor for assistance. As with other black mayors, there were unrealistic expectations coupled with white fears. Latinos quickly made it clear to Dinkins that they were not satisfied with his early appointments. Also, Dinkins's hesitation in addressing the continuing racial incidents involving blacks and Koreans and his seeming favoritism to blacks in these cases brought protests from New York's Asian community and criticism from the U.S. Commission on Civil Rights. Furthermore, conflicts between the black and Jewish communities created a picture of a black mayor who cared little about violence perpetuated against other minority groups (Biles 2001).

Coupled with the mayor's fiscal miscues, he had put himself in a difficult position for reelection. Facing Rudy Giuliani in the 1993 election Dinkins had to answer for four years of increasing racial polarization in the city and budgetary issues. As Giuliani claimed during the campaign, "It is patently clear that he can't manage a riot, he can't manage a boycott, he can't manage a budget, and he can't manage a campaign" (Biles 2001, 145). Race dominated the campaign, and the racial lines were drawn tight as evident in the vote totals. The mayor secured over 90 percent of the black vote and 60 percent of the Latino vote, but did poorly among whites. Giuliani won big victories in white ethnic neighborhoods in the outer boroughs (Biles 2001). Dinkins's reelection loss after only one term was a first for a black mayor of a large U.S. city. The mayor's social and racial problems ended public confidence in him. Dinkins's inability to reconcile competing ethnic and racial groups destroyed his mayoralty.

Other black mayors in similar multiracial cities to Dinkins's New York, were able to stay in power over a long period. In Los Angeles, Tom Bradley succeeded where Dinkins failed. He managed to maintain a diverse racial coalition through a number of terms. Los Angeles was as racially polarized as New York, yet Bradley's electoral coalition was probably the most ethnically and racially diverse coalition of a large city black mayoral candidate up to that time. The 1973 election was his second bid for mayor, having been narrowly defeated in 1969 by Samuel Yorty, a white candidate who capitalized on fears of black militancy and student unrest. Moderation and cross-cultural appeals characterized the 1973 Bradley campaign. On the one hand, Bradley received the support of the large Jewish population which, like blacks, were a cultural and political outgroup (Sonenshein 1986). At the same time his commercials featured him in his police uniform to convey the message that he would maintain community order. He also attempted to mobilize the low income Latino voters as another outgroup. In the end Bradley received 91 percent of the black vote, 46 percent of the white vote, and 51 percent of the Latinos, an impressive multicultural coalition, but racially polarized nonetheless (Hahn et al 1976). As he governed over his five terms, black discontent increased. Unlike Dinkins and the black mayors of majority black cities, Bradley's "color-blind approach to politics and his efforts to distance himself from the black community resulted in some African Americans resenting him for not using his position to pursue their concerns aggressively" (Parker 2001).

Nonetheless, Bradley was a master of coalition politics and maintained support from blacks even as he reached out for the votes of other races. While paying attention to issues that would help the black community such as jobs and housing, he never put it in racial terms. He was careful not to alienate his white supporters, as Dinkins did. Bradley was able to deracialize his programs and spoke not for any one group, but for the city and its people as a whole. The only subgroup not accepting this approach were militant blacks who saw Bradley as somewhat of an "Uncle Tom" for not specifically fighting for black causes. According to one analyst of the mayor's career, his approach was not just politically motivated to maintain his coalition but represented his long-held beliefs about intergroup relations, governance and success in America. He was mayor of all the people in Los Angeles, not just blacks. African Americans, he felt, could find success just as other groups did and cross all barriers just as he did (Parker 2001).

Although it was long a part of the mayor's philosophy, Bradley's emphasis on serving all the people also stemmed from his loss in the mayoral election in 1969 to Yorty. Yorty turned the campaign into a racial conflict and accused Bradley of being a militant who would damage the city and the police department. Rather than provide this type of ammunition to his opponent, Bradley stressed that he would be mayor for all Los Angeles citizens. His effort to eliminate race as a campaign issue served him well especially among white liberals and Jewish voters (Parker 2001).

Bradley was certainly mayor for all Los Angeles residents but at the same time did a good deal to fortify his coalition. He brought a number of blacks, Latinos, and Asians into his administration, supported affirmative action and low-cost housing. Maintaining the coalition was a balancing act that at times led the mayor to support one group over another only to switch back again. Bradley refused to castigate Louis Farrakhan when he arrived in Los Angeles to give a speech, thereby angering Jewish voters. However, the mayor also showed his solidarity with the Jewish community as they protested the Soviet Union's anti-Semitic policies. Holding on to his Jewish supporters was an essential part of Bradley's tactics but at times this brought him into conflict with black constituents. In situations where there was no safe response for the mayor, as with the busing of black children into white neighborhoods, he simply refused to take a stand. As one journalist commented, "Bradley is caught in a high-pressured tug of war between the two groups" (Parker 2001, 168).

For an African American mayor to ignore school busing issues was unusual, but typical for Bradley who understood well that blacks in Los Angeles were a clear minority in numbers and that other groups needed to be appeased. Blacks were urged to vote for the mayor on the basis that he represented a symbolic and, in many cases, a real victory for the community even if he did not do everything the community wanted. Bradley's reelection indicates the success of his balancing act. For other mayors, reelections often meant changes in policy that pulled them away from their initial commitments to the black community.

As Atlanta's mayor Maynard Jackson approached his second term reelection campaign in 1977, racial tensions were still high and many white business leaders remained uncomfortable with a black mayor and black political ascendancy. Business leaders looked frantically for a viable white opponent to Jackson. Faced with continuing hostility from a business community he needed in order to have an economically strong city, Jackson began to tone down his rhetoric and activist policies. A program to target black neighborhoods for funds and improvements took a new turn. Complaints from the business community about using Federal Community Development Block Grants for residential rather than downtown commercial purposes led Jackson to proclaim in 1977 the need for a strong business district and to subsequently use 50 percent of the grant funds for "public works improvements in the downtown area." The downtown section began to take priority (Bayor 2001).

Jackson also pleased the business group with his stand against a sanitation workers' strike in 1977. Shifting from his 1970 rhetoric in which he had backed a similar strike, the mayor sided with white business leaders and middle-class blacks who saw no benefit in supporting a strike by low-income black workers. The firing of almost one thousand low-paid black sanitation employees would not have happened just a few years earlier in this majority black city. An increase in jobs for the low-income and black segment of Atlanta's population also became a low priority for the mayor (Bayor 2001).

Jackson's 1977 reelection was an easy victory but he garnered only 19.5 percent of the white vote, slightly above his total in 1973. But it was not a majority of white votes that he needed. Black voters were his base support, and the white business group was essential to govern and to grow the city economically. Jackson had accomplished much in his first term and was still an important symbolic hero for blacks. However, Jackson's rapprochement with the white business elite set the pattern for future black mayors.

After his 1981 victory, Atlanta's next black mayor, Andrew Young, worked diligently to embrace the business leaders and make them part of his coalition. The reason was clear and reflected Jackson's experience and willingness to shift. As Young said at a luncheon for white business leaders, "I didn't get elected with your help, but I can't govern without you." (Bayor 2001, 189) Young understood that his position as mayor would guarantee that "whites get some of the [political] power and blacks get some of the money" (Bayor 2001, 189). Young would be easily reelected in 1985, but soon would be described by the *Atlanta Constitution* as "the darling of the business community"(Bayor 2001, 190). Black middle-class concerns in regard to affirmative action, the minority business enterprise program, and hiring blacks in the city bureaucracy still held the mayor's attention, but low-income blacks received little notice. Economic development in the downtown areas was the main concern (Bayor 2001, 190).

Much like Bradley in Los Angeles, in Atlanta Young could depend on his black vote, even among the low-income, regardless of some complaints within the group. For the majority of black leaders, including those representing the poor, support for a black mayor was essential and required. Despite Young's policies, or Bradley's, there was little desire to weaken a black mayor or decrease black political power. Poor black neighborhoods were neglected, and hopes for better schools, housing, jobs, and police protection were left unfulfilled. Insurgency, the initial style of a number of black mayors, often faded; compromise and governing became the norm.

Carl Stokes's reelection campaign in Cleveland, a majority white city, showed similarities to both Bradley and Jackson. Sure of his black support, Stokes pitched his campaign to white moderates. He emphasized his ability to deal with racial violence and his probusiness policies. As historian Leonard Moore states, "the support of white moderates and the business community was instrumental in Stokes's victory" in 1969 (2001, 97). However, his second term was mired in police related issues, fiscal problems, and mounting tensions with the city council. This problematic second term convinced Stokes not to seek reelection in 1971; a black mayor was not elected again until 1990 (Moore 2001).

Stokes, like David Dinkins, was not able to hold onto his white supporters. He could not gain control of racial issues that included many aspects of urban life. In Cleveland, where in 1980 blacks were still only 44 percent of the population, white political opponents remained too strong for Stokes. Furthermore, according to Moore, with the easing of racial violence in Cleveland, whites did not see the basic need for a black mayor to put out racial fires. White moderate and business community backing dissipated (Moore 2001).

The racial shift that occurred with the election of black mayors reveals clearly the significance of race in the life of American cities. Into the 1990s, thirty years after the election of the first black mayors, the ascendancy of blacks into city halls still drew hostile reactions from whites. The shift resulted in more turmoil than even the Irish securing the mayor's office in Boston in previous decades. The hostility to ethnic succession paled in regard to racial succession. Governance also was difficult as many whites saw the election of black politicians as a device to get the city through racially violent periods but otherwise did not support the new mayors.

As racial pioneers, black mayors were scrutinized carefully and their mistakes highlighted in ways that white mayors did not have to face. The cities they inherited, particularly in the northern rustbelt, often were declining. The white middle class was moving out, businesses were abandoning the city, the economy was reeling from deindustrialization, schools and city services were declining, and population shifts put large numbers of young blacks in places with few jobs. Ethnic succession had worked relatively well when jobs were plentiful and there was a willingness, for the good of the city or party, to share power (Adler 2001, 2–3). As blacks moved to the head of the line, there was little desire on the part of whites to share power and the perks of governing had largely disappeared in these collapsing cities.

Campaigns with a black candidate for mayor often turned into racial attacks. Polarization was evident in many of these cities. The black vote was crucial to electing black mayors in a number of situations. Even in multiracial cities such as New York and Los Angeles, the core black vote was a necessary part of a winning coalition (although Bradley did not always acknowledge this fact). In these types of situations, in which blacks form only a relatively small part of the electorate, black candidates usually have tried to de-emphasize their race. Most white and Latino voters did not want to hear what the black mayor would do for the black community; they wanted to hear how the city's problems would be handled in a nonbiased manner. Bradley was particularly skillful at deracializing his campaigns and administrations. Dinkins was not and as a result served only one term.

In majority black cities, the balancing act was different. Maynard Jackson did not need many white voters to win and could be aggressive in changing the racial atmosphere in Atlanta. However, he needed the white business leaders to govern and therefore had to lessen the insurgent positions he first took. Winning an election was only the first hurdle; governing required compromise and coalitions. Jackson and Young were eventually able to largely disregard low-income black demands as they sought to work with the white business elite and the black middle class. Eventually class trumps race if the black mayor can represent the city's economic interests, of both the white and black communities, in a successful fashion.

Mayors usually cannot change very much and hostile state legislators or recalcitrant city councils easily diminish their power. However, in the case of black mayors, conditions were often so dismal for the black community under earlier white mayors that any change would be a significant improvement. Even in deracialized administrations, the opening up of jobs in the city bureaucracy, the use of black owned firms in city work, and the effort to control police brutality were major steps forward, but they did not solve all problems. Maynard Jackson said that the black community and its concerns were always on his mind, always on his daily agenda of thought (Bayor 1996). This interest was usually not evident in the thinking of white mayors, and therefore the black community, whether in New York, Los Angeles or Atlanta, was often ignored. This new interest represented the most important shift.

Notable, too, is that some black mayors entered city halls in well-working cities with strong economies and served their terms as these cities grew even more prosperous. Urban centers such as Seattle, Denver, and Spokane had very small black populations but were able to transcend race to support black candidates and subsequent mayors who promised a continued strong economy (Colburn 2001).

This general look at cities across the United States only reveals the complexity of recognizing and understanding patterns in the rise of blacks to political prominence. The next chapter offers a closer look at the four cities that are the focus of this research—Detroit, New Orleans, Chicago, and Charlotte. In these cities, with black majorities in Detroit and New Orleans, a multiethnic population in Chicago and a majority white citizenry in Charlotte, we can observe a rich racial history surrounding mayoral politics.

Chapter 3
Mayoral Racial History in Four Cities

Chapter Authored by Ronald H. Bayor and Huey L. Perry

The four cities examined in this research—Detroit, New Orleans, Chicago, and Charlotte—reveal the centrality of mayoral politics in racial polarization. The campaigns and the governance of both the white and black mayors in these citites set the tone for how race and politics were mutually affective and how racial conflict emerged.

Detroit

Detroit prospered economically during World War II by filling government orders for military supplies and equipment. After the war, the Detroit auto industry regained its position as the main economic driver in the city. But, with the advent of automation, and the spread of auto industry jobs to other cities, employment opportunities in that industry eventually decreased. Foreign competition accelerated the decrease, leading to high unemployment rates in the city.

Even before these economic changes, Detroit was already characterized by racial polarization. As was the typical discrimination pattern in rustbelt cities, blacks were concentrated in unskilled, low-paying jobs in the factories and unions. Strong racial discrimination was evident by the fact that many blacks were employed in positions that were below their abilities and skills. In addition, more young African Americans were migrating from the South into the city just as employment in the auto factories and related industries was disappearing. Housing was another area of strong segregation. And Detroit's political leaders turned a blind eye to long-standing police brutality (Rich 1989), which only increased racial animosity. All of the above created a high level of frustration among blacks which ultimately resulted in race riots in 1943 and 1967.

Detroit was undergoing demographic changes as a result of white flight and black in-migration. These demographic changes portended political change. The city went from 20 percent black in 1955 to 44 percent in 1970, to 63 percent in 1980 and to 76 percent black in 1990 (Welch 2001; Thompson 2001). Unexpectedly, Jerome Cavanaugh, the city's first liberal mayor, was elected in 1961, defeating incumbent Louis Miriani. Believing that Miriani was a sure winner, the business community and the United Auto Workers of Detroit endorsed him. However, the liberal Cavanaugh won in an upset because he was able to obtain the support of the black community by promising black leaders a role in his new administration (Rich 1991); his winning electoral coalition was made up of black voters and middle class whites.

Cavanaugh's administration was characterized by outreach to help the black community. One example of this outreach was the revived Committee on Community Relations that was charged with enforcing fair employment practices in firms with city contracts. Second, Cavanaugh appointed several African Americans to positions in his cabinet, such as Alfred Pelham, city comptroller and George Edwards, commissioner of police. It is difficult to underestimate the impact of these appointments. The police and city finances are arguably the most critical areas of urban governance, and, in Detroit, under Cavanaugh, blacks headed both. And finally, Cavanaugh was the first white mayor of a large majority white city to appoint a black police chief.

However, even though blacks in Detroit were comparatively better off than blacks in other cities, the huge socioeconomic gap between whites and blacks in Detroit remained. The disadvantaged position of blacks in Detroit was evident in their lower incomes, higher unemployment, and lower levels of education. The reforms of the new liberal mayor could not erase the most basic problems faced by black residents: housing shortages, loss of industrial jobs, and concentrations of poverty in dysfunctional neighborhoods. The result was that many members of the black community felt disenfranchised and impatient about the lack of change in their daily lives. This ultimately led to militancy in the black community (Herman 2002, 6).

Militant leaders like the Reverend Albert Cleague and H. Rap Brown argued that whites would never voluntarily share power with blacks, and called for more aggressive action, including black separatism. At a black power rally in Detroit in early 1967, H. Rap Brown stated that if "Motown" didn't come around, "we are going to burn you down" (Herman 2002, 6). These threats were made in the context of a mayor who was making a genuine effort to improve the lives of blacks and to include them in city government. But the frustrations borne of years of discrimination and poverty could not be satisfied with the incremental reforms of one mayor, and the rise of militancy could not be stopped.

Housing was the most critical problem facing blacks in Detroit. Before the 1967 riots, the lack of affordable housing was the uppermost concern of black residents. When polled by the *Detroit Free Press* regarding the problems that contributed most to the 1967 riots, respondents listed "poor housing" as one of the most important issues, second only to police brutality (Thomas 1997, 130–31). The housing problem served as a flashpoint for black militancy because the cost and quality of housing for blacks was quite different from the cost and quality of housing for whites. This obvious and visible disparity exacerbated the frustration blacks in Detroit felt because of racial discrimination.

As in many other cities, public housing was the only viable alternative for those who could not afford private housing, and in Detroit public housing was highly segregated as well as densely populated, "reinforcing isolation by race and income and reducing informal supervision over children and youth" (Thomas 1997, 26–27). Even with these undesirable conditions there were more applications for public housing than there were available units. The city displaced blacks when run-down, low-income housing was demolished in the name of progress, relocating the occupants to dense housing projects (Sugrue 1996). This was the 1960s style of "urban renewal" across most of America.

The generations of systemic discrimination blacks experienced erupted in the 1967 race riots. During this period the National Guard was called in, and the city appeared to be out of control as people roamed the streets and numerous fires broke out. This was the lowest point in race relations in the history of Detroit. Following the riots, white out-migration to the suburbs accelerated, which assured that Detroit would be majority black (Rich 1991). Wilbur Rich describes the change in Detroit's governing coalition as follows:

> Detroit's political environment had become completely unbalanced. The Irish and Polish politicians lost their power base because their fellow ethnics dispersed into the suburbs. The rampant flight of ethnic groups left a minority of liberals, small pockets of Southern immigrants, and elderly residents as the remaining white population. The 1970 Census found that the black population had risen to 44 percent of the city's population (Rich 1991, 66).

Throughout the 1970s, many American cities began experiencing a shift from majority white to majority black when whites fled to the suburbs leaving the central cities to African Americans. Following the 1967 riots, white citizens tended to view Detroit as a city in decline and blamed the black community for its problems. By contrast, in a 1971 survey the new black majority expressed optimism about the future of the city, and even optimism about race relations (Rich 1991).

With a new black majority it was only a matter of time before an African American became the chief executive of Detroit. Black and other voters almost elected the first black mayor in 1969, but Richard Austin lost the mayoral election by one percentage point. However, the city was ready for change, which came in 1973 with the election of Detroit's first black mayor Coleman A. Young. The dominant issue in the 1973 mayoral campaign was police brutality against blacks, stemming from the feeling among blacks that police brutality was the main cause of the 1967 riots. The white candidate, John Nichols, was the former police commissioner who defended police behavior during the riots. The black candidate, Young, was highly critical of the police, echoing the sentiments of most black voters. Voting turnout in twenty-three key precincts for the 1973 mayoral runoff election shows that Young won thirteen of the twenty-three districts. As expected, this was a racially polarized election. With few exceptions, Young won the black districts and Nichols won the white districts. Young also won the two racially mixed districts (Rich 1989, 105).

When Young became Detroit's first black mayor in 1974, he realized that the city's salvation lay in a truce that would reverse the trend of white businesses relocating to the suburbs. During his first speech after taking his oath of office, Young stated, "we can no longer afford the luxury of hatred and racial division. What is good for the black people of this city is good for the white people. . . . What is good for those who live in the suburbs is good for those of us who live in the central city" (Jacoby 1998, 297). However, the city faced enormous financial problems at that time and Mayor Young chose to cut the police department budget. Subsequently, Detroit's crime problem accelerated, and the city became an almost lawless zone, producing even more white flight. Thus, Young failed in his downtown economic development efforts, and economic problems continued to plague his entire tenure as mayor (Jacoby 1998).

Young's administration was characterized by hostile relationships with the surrounding suburbs, a common phenomenon for black mayors. Such hostile relationships did not exist prior to his administration, and they highlighted the racial divide between the majority black city and the majority white suburbs. Mayor Young also exhibited a sort of zero tolerance toward community organizations within the city that did not support him. In the words of one community activist, "If you supported the mayor it was great when Coleman was in office, because you were assured of getting money. The reverse was also true, however. Community-based organizations that did not support him were completely cut off from city funding and services" (Parr 1998, 3).

As anticipated by the black community, Young became a champion of civil rights issues. Two issues that Mayor Young was particularly interested in were police brutality and minority contracts. He immediately set out to integrate the Detroit Police Department by appointing three black men and one white man to the police commission. One of the units within the department was an undercover crime program with a reputation for abusive treatment of blacks (Rich 1989). Mayor Young abolished this unit. Regarding minority contracts, programs called "set aside programs" were established in many American cities in the 1970s. They allotted a certain amount of a city's contract business to minority-owned businesses. Although these programs were controversial, they were also very successful (Chay and Fairlie 1998). Detroit's specific version of minority set-aside programs was designed to address past discrimination in the awarding of city contracts by giving Minority Business Enterprises (MBEs) greater participation in city contracts (Bates and Williams 1995).

Given his emphasis on civil rights, racial conflict characterized all of Young's five elections, even when he ran against other African American candidates in runoff elections. White voters supported Young's opponents because of their intense dissatisfaction with Young, their loss of power and status, conditions in the city, and racism. Young was elected all five times by a coalition consisting overwhelmingly of blacks, about 10 percent of whites, and parts of the business community. For twenty years the Young administrations were racially divisive, continuing a history of racial polarization that existed since the first race riot in 1943.

Young did not run for reelection in 1993. This campaign was a contest between two candidates: Sharon McPhail, who represented Young's confrontational style, and Michigan Supreme Court Justice Dennis Archer, who advocated a collaborative approach to governance. Archer's electoral coalition was the racial opposite of Young's, consisting of virtually the entire white vote and only a slight majority of the black vote. Archer prevailed over McPhail with 57 percent of the vote. This change of administration marked an economic and civic renaissance for Detroit because it brought about such a dramatic shift in governance style at city hall. "Instead of confronting the rest of the region, or forcing political loyalty from a neighborhood group before working with it, or challenging private sector leaders, Archer used a diplomatic approach" (Parr 1998). As a result, he won reelection in 1997 in a landslide with 83 percent of the vote.

Similar to other large, majority African American cities, Detroit had a split leadership structure, with blacks controlling city hall and city politics, and whites controlling the economic system. Archer reformed this split system and established a more inclusive civic decision-making process. His initiative inspired leaders of Detroit's white civic organizations and foundations to also open their decision-making processes to African Americans (Parr 1998).

Archer also made several substantive accomplishments during his mayoral tenure, most of which related to economic development in the downtown area. During his administration two new professional sports stadiums were built downtown and a suburban computer company relocated to the city (Montemurri 2001). Probably the signature economic development achievement was the decision of General Motors to relocate its world headquarters into the once much-maligned Renaissance Center. David Littmann, Chief Economist for Detroit-based Comerica Bank, believes that none of these business developments could have occurred if Young had still been mayor. Littmann states: "You have to credit the [Archer] administration not only with having a better attitude toward business, but with really relentless efforts to move businesses into the heart of Detroit" (Gurwitt 2000).

There were several major disappointments during Archer's mayoral tenure, most of which reflect the problems black mayors generally encounter. Under Archer's watch the police and fire departments experienced serious problems. The most serious of these was the continuing problem of alleged police abuse of citizens. Also, many neighborhoods remained blighted, and the city's population fell below one million for the 2000 census. As seen in other cities, the problems black mayors inherit are often overwhelming. Detroit's changing economy, deindustrialization, and the sagging fortunes of the auto industry along with new administrations in Washington less generous to cities, preordained difficult times for Detroit's mayors.

New Orleans

While the politics of New Orleans and Detroit are similar in some important ways, the two cities have very different economic bases. New Orleans' economy is based on tourism, whereas Detroit's economy is based on automotive manufacturing. This has been the basis of the two cities' economies for more than seventy years. The different economies of the two cities have had enormous implications for the composition of their populations. Detroit is a city of immigrants whereas New Orleans' population consists mainly of Louisianians who moved to the city from smaller cities, towns, and rural areas.

According to the United States Census Report of 1960 the population of New Orleans was 37.2 percent black. By 1970, New Orleans was 45 percent black; 1980, 55 percent; and 1990, 62 percent. In the 1960, 1970, and 1980 censuses the highest reported employment category for black males was laborer, and for black females it was private household worker. This did not substantially change until the 1990 census when the highest employment category for blacks was professional and related services, such as hospitals and health services (Hirsch, 2001).

The emergence of black political power in New Orleans coincided with a transformation of white mayoral leadership that was typical in the post civil rights era South. Prior to the emergence of black political power in southern cities, white mayors were racially conservative. Therefore, the first white mayor who black leaders attempted to negotiate with for more resources for the black community was racially conservative. As blacks increased their voter registration rates, they were able to form a coalition with a small number of moderate and liberal whites. As the black and white components of the racial coalition increased over time, the coalition was first able to elect a racially moderate white mayor, followed by a racially liberal white mayor, which was followed by an African-American mayor (Perry 1997, 1990).

DeLesseps Story "Chep" Morrison was a "reformer" in New Orleans' political history and served as mayor from 1946-1961. Although he was a segregationist, Morrison was pragmatic and successfully appealed to A.P. Tureaud, the leader of the New Orleans Branch of the National Association for the Advancement of Colored People (NAACP) to not file civil rights lawsuits against the city during his mayoral campaign. By not forcing civil rights issues that Morrison would have had to address, Tureaud allowed Morrison to avoid being perceived as "problack" by whites in the city, nor did he appear to the black community to be "antiblack." In order to be reelected, Morrison needed both white and black support, and he adroitly managed to appear as an advocate of both groups. Tureaud understood Morrison's desire to maintain racial tranquility in New Orleans and once stated that he "didn't do a whole lot for Negroes [other than to] stimulate their desire to participate in politics" (Hirsch 1992, 279).

Morrison's contributions to the black community included symbolic contributions, such as speaking before black audiences where he announced that he was "the mayor of all the people" (Haas 1974, 68) In public he advocated for social justice, but in private he supported segregation. In 1950 Morrison agreed to the recruitment of two blacks to the New Orleans Police Department, "with the private understanding that they were to operate in Negro areas only" (Fairclough 1995, 153). The limitation to black areas only was to assure that no white person suffered the indignity of being arrested by a black police officer.

Blacks also received several more substantive gains during the Morrison administration; the most important of which was the creation of the New Orleans Recreation Department (NORD). The NORD programs were the first chance that black children had to participate in public athletic activities. Morrison also provided blacks access to new playgrounds, recreational complexes, and new public swimming pools. In addition to NORD, Morrison was instrumental in repairing streets in black neighborhoods and building public housing complexes (Haas 1974).

Victor Hugo Schiro served as New Orleans mayor from 1961 until 1970. Schiro was considered a hardcore segregationist, openly associated with the White Citizens Council, and generally ignored black voters. Schiro did, however, encourage many integrationist programs because behind the scenes the white power structure was urging these steps to prevent civil unrest (Fairclough 1995, 282). Perhaps the most important issue that Schiro faced during his administration was the integration of public schools. Schiro prepared for the integration of New Orleans' public schools in the early 1960s under the threat of possible litigation and with the advice of New Orleans' white business leaders. Blacks were hired for the first time as bus drivers for New Orleans Public Services, Inc. (NOPSI) to stave off a boycott from bus riders and their supporters. Schiro was also responsible for the removal of racial signs from City Hall and for black sanitation men and firemen being hired.

Schiro was reelected mayor in 1965 with endorsements from several prominent black leaders despite the fact that his opponent made stronger appeals for black support as well as accurately portraying Schiro as a segregationist. So, although Schiro was reelected, he only received between one-quarter and one-third of the black vote. The 1965 election marked the beginning of substantial black electoral power in New Orleans mayoral politics (Fairclough 1995).

But New Orleans was not ready for a black mayor yet. In 1970 Maurice "Moon" Landrieu was elected as New Orleans' first white liberal mayor. He received a large portion of the African American vote and endorsements from the major black political organizations. However, consistent with the racial polarization pattern, he received only a minority of the white vote (Fairclough 1995, 427). This was the first time in New Orleans' political history that black voters had determined the outcome of a mayoral election.

Landrieu immediately began to reform city politics to include African Americans. He appointed blacks to key positions in city government, including several heads of city departments, an executive assistant, and a chief administrative officer—the top appointed position in city government. Landrieu's realized that the growing black vote in New Orleans could be part of a winning majority biracial coalition.

The mobilization of black voters during the Landrieu administrations, along with the increasing percentage of black voters in the city, set the stage for the election of the first black mayor of New Orleans, Ernest "Dutch"

Morial in 1977. As with other cities' first black mayors, Morial encountered intense racial opposition to his mayoral candidacy. Morial could be confident of his black support, but since the city was still majority white, he could not win without substantial white support as well. In his campaign, Morial promoted the ideal of a single society open to all on the basis of merit. However, two of the city's powerful black political organizations were not pleased with this theme since their survival depended on a racial divide and high levels of race consciousness among blacks (Hirsch 1998). Yet, a third black political organization set itself up to mediate between black and white interests in city politics, occupying a middle ground as black leaders who enjoyed and were enamored with white political support. Thus, some African American leaders served as political brokers bridging the relationship between the African-American community and the white political leaders (Hirsch 1998)

The 1977 primary election for mayor of New Orleans was highly polarized by race. Morial finished first in the primary, followed by Joe DiRosa. Morial received 58 percent of the black vote and 5 percent of the white vote, while DiRosa secured 39 percent of the white and only 4 percent of the black vote. Even with Morial in the race, black turnout in the primary was eight percentage points less than that of whites (Perry and Stokes, 1987). The runoff election was a similar story, but with less racial polarization. Morial entered the runoff fully knowledgeable that he could not win the election with support from African American voters alone; he also needed more support from white voters. Blacks comprised only 41.6 percent of the registered electorate for this primary election (King 1977). In the runoff Morial ran a more deracialized campaign. Morial employed a dual strategy, dictated by the differences between a primary election and a runoff election, to become New Orleans' first African American mayor. This deracialized strategy paid off as Morial won the runoff election with 95 percent of the African American vote and 19 percent of the white vote, totaling to 51.7 percent of total votes cast. A key ingredient in Morial's victory was the increased interest that blacks manifested in the electoral process following his entry into the runoff.

Another key to Morial's victory was the fact that he received almost 20 percent of the white vote. Twenty percent is the upper end of the range of support from white voters that most successful black candidates running for public office in biracial political jurisdictions can hope to receive; 10 percent is the lower end of the range. Thus, Morial's ability to win 19 percent of the white vote was clearly an impressive accomplishment (Perry and Stokes 1987).

Similar to Young's situation in Detroit, Morial faced a poor city with African Americans who had unrealistic expectations of what a black mayor could do for them. The economic problems in New Orleans were deep and included low levels of education, underemployment, unemployment, poverty, and a large income gap between the poor and the middle class (Schexnider 1982). In addition, the city depended upon federal and state funds for 57 percent of its operating budget. Under President Ronald Reagan federal funds coming into New Orleans were drastically cut by 47 percent which caused federal and state aid to be only 30 percent of the city's operating budget (Popkin 1981).

Mayor Morial's achievements included both economic development efforts and greater inclusion of blacks in city affairs. He cut employees and expenses at city hall to the point where the budget was balanced, and he was instrumental in attracting major business and retail developments to the downtown area. To include African Americans he set aside 10 percent of city contacts for minority business entrepreneurs and created New Orleans' first office of minority business development.

In spite of these achievements, white voters, and especially business leaders, became more discontented with his administration. One possible explanation is that Morial was confrontational rather than being a consensus builder (Perry 2003). As Perry notes, "Morial asserted that he was pro-economic development and that he had no problem with the business community in its entirety—only with certain business leaders" (2003,184). According to Morial, his problem with those leaders involved whether the city should play a substantive role in economic development or should the city let the private sector handle this development.

Although Morial won reelection in 1982, the campaign was more racially polarized than his first election. Running against a white opponent, he received only 8 percent of the white vote, which was 11 percent fewer than he received four years before. This was a surprisingly low showing since the city's major white newspaper endorsed his candidacy.

Morial's confrontational style set the stage for the next mayor, Sidney Barthelemy, a mild mannered decidedly nonconfrontational executive. By 1986 the New Orleans electorate was majority black, but the white voters clearly wanted a less aggressive black mayor than Morial. In a runoff against black State Senator William Jefferson, Barthelemy received most of the white vote, making him essentially the "white" candidate in a black on black election. Then four years later, when he ran against a respected white community leader, he received only 21 percent of the white vote, changing his identity to the "black candidate." Thus, Barthelemy's racial identity in the eyes of the voters reversed depending on the opponent.

The eight-year-long Barthelemy administration was generally acknowledged as a failure. The impact of declining revenues and a declining population began to be felt in the quality of life (Howell 1994). Crack cocaine had been introduced, and the city was experiencing an unprecedented murder rate. The most severe blow to the city's economy was the pullout or cutbacks of major oil companies in the wake of the 1980s "oil bust." The petrochemical industry had been the backbone of New Orleans' economy, and there was little diversification in the economy to diminish the impact of the loss of oil jobs. While Barthelemy was not responsible for these events, he seemed at a loss as to how to deal with them.

The 1994 mayoral contest was set against the backdrop of years of unprecedented high crime rates, especially murder rates. Marc Morial, son of Dutch Morial, was the major black candidate, and Donald Mintz, the same white community leader who challenged Barthelemy, was the major white candidate. This campaign was highly racial, with Morial suggesting that "only his election would stop the white challenge to the 16-year Black control of city hall" (Liu 2005, 71). He received only 3 percent of the white vote in the most racially polarized election in New Orleans history (Engstrom and Kirkland 1995, 6). Morial began his administration with an overhaul of the corrupt and dysfunctional Police Department. The result was a steady decline in murders for several successive years and increased optimism among citizens about the quality of life in New Orleans (Howell 1998, 2000). He also revitalized NORD, which resulted in improved playgrounds and parks, which had fallen victim to the city's financial woes. During his administration, three major economic development projects were completed: the expansion of the Morial Convention Center (named for his father), which was accompanied by a large increase in the number of downtown hotels, and the opening of a casino.

The most consistent criticism of his administration was an overdeveloped system of patronage wherein friends and relatives were rewarded with lucrative city contracts. This criticism was leveled primarily by white voters who saw the system as a misuse of city funds and the absence of merit in the contracting process. On the other hand, many black enterprises were the beneficiaries of this system. Patronage aside, Morial remained a fairly popular mayor throughout his administration, ranging from a 47 percent to 59 percent approval among whites and a 72 percent to 91 percent approval among blacks (Howell 2002).

Chicago

Chicago is a city with a long history of machine politics, a powerful political boss in Mayor Richard J. Daley, and black politicians who worked with the machine but derived little from it for their black constituents.

Blacks have been a minority population in this multiethnic city. Early on, they were confined to segregated sections of the city and any efforts to move elsewhere were met with white violence and white flight. In 1959, the U.S. Commission on Civil Rights designated this city as America's "most residentially segregated city" (Biles 1995). Furthermore, as in other cities, police brutality was an issue, and blacks were underrepresented on the police force—a situation that continued into the 1990s (Illinois Advisory Committee 1993). It was, in essence, a racially polarized city under white mayors, and more so when Harold Washington, the first black mayor, was elected in 1983.

Daley, who claimed on a number of occasions that Chicago had no ghettos, consistently favored his white ethnic supporters. The city's blacks were part of the machine's coalition and loyal to Daley. In the 1963 election, Chicago blacks gave Daley 81 percent of their vote (Cohen and Taylor 2000). Part of their steadfastness was due to a misguided sense that the Democrats helped them get public housing and welfare (Biles 1995). The mayor also maintained black support through patronage and organizational control (Cohen and Taylor 2000). As a result, Daley offered little to this group in any meaningful way in regard to housing, school segregation, or police brutality, but did at times provide minor benefits to blacks through appointments. Policies that would lose white votes were not enacted (Biles 1995).

Daley had the perfect situation for his machine's longevity but it was not a perfect situation for the city. Integration came slowly and black demands for Benjamin Willis, the superintendent of schools, to be fired got nowhere even after boycotts were initiated during the early 1960s. Although black politicians on the Southside did not challenge the system, due to personally benefiting from the machine, the black community did rise up in protest through boycotts and a riot that lasted four days in August 1965. Daley remained uninterested and continued to claim that there were no civil rights problems in Chicago (Biles 1995; Cohen and Taylor 2000).

Chicago was a city on the edge of further racial outbursts and led by a mayor who could or would not see this. When Martin Luther King, Jr. came to Chicago to protest housing segregation, he faced a mayor who appeared conciliatory but subsequently would do as little as possible. King also demanded the end of job bias and the establishment of a civilian review board to address police brutality issues (Cohen and Taylor 2000). A three-day riot in the summer of 1966, for which the Illinois National Guard was needed to quell the riot, further illustrated the severe racial tensions in the city. As King marched through insular white neighborhoods, he and the other demonstrators were viciously attacked by white mobs (Biles 1995). King's comment, "I've been in many demonstrations all across the south, but I can say that I have never seen—even in Mississippi and Alabama—mobs as hostile and hate-filled as I've seen in Chicago, I think the people from Mississippi ought to come to Chicago to learn how to hate" (Cohen and Taylor 2000, 396), reveals the extent of white hostility that King faced in Chicago. Through sleight-of-hand maneuvers, Daley seemed to be complying with King's demands, but had no follow through, so housing segregation remained.

Daley's actions did not hurt him politically. He continued to maintain both his white and black support and was reelected in 1967 with 73 percent of the vote (Biles 1995). The mayor controlled his black constituency through black leaders in the ghetto area and controlled his "bungalow belt," working class white constituency by preventing housing integration (Cohen and Taylor 2000). The isolation of blacks politically and residentially continued. Also, conditions in black neighborhoods did not improve. When the courts ordered the city to build new public housing in white areas rather than concentrating them in black sections of the city, Daley simply stopped the construction of any new public housing developments (Biles 1995). As one study of Daley notes, the mayor was particularly adept at appearing to be concerned about civil rights issues (Cohen and Taylor 2000). Politically, although not ethically, Daley's moves were correct if he wanted to maintain his machine as it was. Housing integration would have spread the black population into other parts of the city and away from the tight control of Daley's black subordinates. At the same time, it would have hastened white flight, therefore losing his white base to the suburbs (Cohen and Taylor 2000).

The Daley years of racial polarization and violence continued the impact of race in politics. Chicago was beginning to lose its white population and gaining more blacks and Latinos. In the 1960s, Chicago gained 300,000 blacks and lost 570,000 whites (Cohen and Taylor 2000). The voting age population rose from 20.2 percent black and 5.6 percent Latino in 1960 to 34.1 percent black and 22.7 percent Latino in 2000, while the white voting age population fell from 79.7 percent to 46.2 percent during the same period. It was clear that a biracial or multiracial coalition was needed in Chicago.

Mayor Daley had considerable black support, which, according to one student of Chicago politics, began to decline as middle class blacks became less willing to support the machine. After Daley died in 1976, Michael Bilandic, a machine politician, was named as acting mayor. Bilandic continued Daley's treatment of blacks and refused to deal with discrimination in the police and fire departments (Kleppner 1985). Nonetheless, in the 1977 primary, Bilandic received 47.2 percent of the black vote and in 1979, Jane Byrne, a machine candidate posing as a reformer, won eleven out of twelve black wards (Cohen and Taylor 200). Byrne made a major effort to win the black vote and to point out Bilandic's and the machine's neglect.

The African American vote was a significant part of her election (Kleppner 1985). The racial shift came unexpectedly in 1983 with Harold Washington, one of the politicians who had run against Bilandic in 1977 in the Democratic primary for mayor. The 1983 campaign pitted the incumbent mayor Jane Byrne against Richard M. Daley, son of the late mayor, as the two major candidates in the race. Although Washington was not considered a major contender, he won with 36 percent of the vote as Byrne and Daley split the white vote. Washington also secured 85 percent of the black vote (Hirsch 2001).

Chicago's intense racial polarization was evident in the effort by many Democrats to deny Washington the victory in the general election for mayor. The campaign featured strong racial appeals. The Republican candidate, Bernard Epton attracted much more support and assistance than Republicans would normally attract in Chicago. Washington won with 51.6 percent of the vote in a racially divisive campaign by securing the multiracial coalition he needed. He received approximately 12 percent of the white vote, 62 percent of the Latino vote, and about 98 percent of the black vote (Kleppner 1985).

Although he promised to heal the city and deal with racial fears, continued opposition from Democratic machine politicians who would not accept an African American as mayor marred Washington's mayoralty (Kleppner 1985). He was fought on every occasion from appointments to policy initiatives, especially the placement of public housing projects in white neighborhoods (Kleppner 1985). Beyond race, there was little desire from white city council members and other politicians to upset the status quo. Nonetheless, Washington prevailed and amid the fear and expectations many had at his election, he did manage to weaken the machine (Colburn and Adler 2001). However, as with other black mayors, he was not able to improve the lives of low-income blacks. These Chicago citizens still lived in areas of concentrated poverty and were "isolated from employment and business opportunities" (Chicago Urban League 1991). Deindustralization, the administration in Washington, DC, the movement of jobs to suburbia, as well as the neglect of blacks in the Richard J. Daley years led to continued problems for blacks in Chicago.

In 1987, Washington won the primary with 53.5 percent of the vote and the general election with 53.7 percent of the vote. Perhaps in his second term, Washington could have accomplished more, but soon after his reelection, he died. The city council selected Alderman Eugene Sawyer, an African American, as mayor. Arnold Hirsch, a historian of Chicago politics, describes Sawyer as "a compliant, black machine operative" (Hirsch 2001, 123). This machine choice split the coalition that Washington had developed and put the machine back in power. A special 1989 election for mayor indicated divisions among the black voters between Sawyer and another black candidate, Alderman Tim Evans. Latino voters, who had supported Washington in his victories, threw their support to Richard M. Daley. Daley won the primary and general election with white and Latino support but received only 3.6 percent of the black vote in the general election (Browning, Marshall, and Tabb 2003). While black support for Daley increased in 1991 (to 22 percent black vote in the general election), blacks no longer had the power evident during Washington's mayoral tenure.

Charlotte

This city was one in which blacks were also a minority—30 percent of Charlotte's population in 1970 and 33 percent in 2000. The city had annexed its suburbs by 2000 and greatly increased its white demographic. However, a united black community could be politically effective when whites were split on issues and candidates. There was also a coalition formed between white business leaders and black political leaders, much like Atlanta before the period of black ascendancy; economic growth issues brought the two groups together (Smith 2004).

Stan Brookshire, the white candidate of the business elite, won the 1961 mayoralty with strong support from blacks. The business community had been willing to support certain aspects of the civil rights movement during Brookshire's first term, allowing the mayor to maintain his popularity in black areas through the 1960s (Smith 2004).

However, as in the other bastion of sunbelt growth, Atlanta, the goals of the business community often did not help low-income blacks. Urban renewal is an example. As a strong supporter of downtown development, Brookshire was active in destroying black neighborhoods in the name of urban renewal. The housing that was razed for commercial structures and recreational areas was not replaced, and blacks were pushed into white working-class sections of the city, causing a racial transition (Hanchett 1998).

Brookshire was willing to break down some racial barriers—he desegregated downtown restaurants, and spoke about providing jobs and housing—but this did not include anything that would seemingly cause problems for the business elite. As a result, the mayor focused on ending the civil rights marches in Charlotte and preventing any bad publicity that would harm the city's image (Smith 2004).

Brookshire supported blacks who shared his gradualist approach to racial change. Two black activists were Reginald Hawkins, who backed demonstrations, and Fred Alexander, a more conciliatory leader who was in favor of holding talks with the white political and business leaders. Brookshire appointed Alexander to the Community Relations Commission, indicating his approval of a go-slow effort. The business community followed through with a policy of providing "loans to black businesses and investments in politically and economically strategic projects" (Smith 2004). Black business leaders were cultivated so as to win votes and cause as little civil rights turmoil as possible. It was a strategy other cities had employed so as not to scare away northern investments or to create a negative national image (Smith 2004).

John Belk, another white mayor, was Brookshire's successor who followed the business strategy to peaceful race relations. Both Brookshire and Belk had been chairmen of the Chamber of Commerce and clearly reflected its point of view. The white business and black political coalition remained strong into the 1980s with the election of Charlotte's first black mayor, Harvey Gantt, in 1983 (Smith 2004). As testimony to the strength of this coalition, Gantt received 29 percent of the white vote (J. Murrey Atkins Library 1987). As one analyst of Charlotte politics states, "By making Charlotte the first large Southern city with a majority white population to elect an African American to the mayor's office, Gantt's victory contributed to Charlotte's reputation as a progressive, racially liberal southern city" (Smith 2004).

As a sunbelt mayor, Gantt was most interested in economic growth although he did increase the number of black companies getting city contracts. Blacks generally did not prosper as much as whites under both liberal white mayors and Gantt. The poverty rate for blacks in 1990 in Mecklenburg County was 21.9 percent as compared to 4.9 percent for whites. However, this county showed a more significant decrease in the poverty difference between blacks and whites than other North Carolina counties in the 1970–2000 period (Smith 2004).

School desegregation was another issue for Charlotte. In an effort to include the suburbs in integration plans, Charlotte and Mecklenburg county schools consolidated in 1960, bringing a long court fight over desegregation and busing that went to the U.S. Supreme Court. The business leaders in Charlotte, in keeping with their desire to maintain the image of a racially fair city, pushed for the desegregation of public places and schools. Under the slogan, "The City That Made It Work," business and black leaders labored to keep Charlotte economically viable. While sparing Charlotte some of the turmoil other southern cities faced, the end result was the same in the eventual resegregation of its schools (Smith 2004).

Gantt was reelected in 1985 but this was his last term in office, losing in 1987 to Sue Myrick, a Republican. Gantt's administration ushered in a period of Republican control and the end of the coalition between business interests and the black community. The mayoral winners since 1987 did not carry the black areas. Republican mayor, Pat McCrory, who was mayor during the data collection for this book, was elected six times beginning in 1995. In the two elections surrounding this research, 1999 and 2001, a black woman, Ella Scarborough, opposed him. In those elections, the typical racial polarization was evident with McCrory receiving 2 percent and 14 percent of the black vote, respectively (Scarborough 2006).

What is evident in these four cities is the different approaches the various mayors and mayoral candidates used for election, and the racial polarization in the vote. Detroit and New Orleans, both of which became majority black cities, saw the election of African American mayors as the cities approached a black population majority. Whites never made up a significant portion of the winning totals in electing black mayors.

In Chicago, the long-term strategy of the machine and its boss Richard J. Daley was to keep blacks as a minor partner in the Democratic Party's election successes and governing. This was a difficult city for blacks to win a place and the eventual election of a black mayor was the result of conflict within the machine and two white candidates splitting the white vote. Racial polarization played a major role in this city's elections. The machine's strength is revealed in its ability to regain control after Washington's death and bring a white mayor back into city hall.

Charlotte, a business run, image conscious city saw a benefit in projecting its racially moderate image. Gantt's election was a natural progression for the Chamber of Commerce. Gantt was, as Maynard Jackson and Andrew Young in Atlanta, and Dennis Archer in Detroit, a voice for the business community. However, in Charlotte, the growth of southern Republicanism and a politicized Christian right eventually reestablished the racial divide through the election of Republican mayors.

For all of these cities, regardless of whether the mayor is an insurgent black, a business-oriented black, a working class white, or a Republican white, racial polarization is still a part of the cities' political, economic, and social life.

Chapter 4
Conducting the Four City Study

Studying politics at the local level is not a simple matter. It is the classic choice between the broad based sample and the in-depth case study. If the researcher chooses a national sample of people in cities, the results have scientific rigor, but probably miss many of the details that flesh out the story in particular locales. In addition, national samples can be overloaded with respondents from the larger cities, so results from a few cities may be driving the conclusions. On the other hand, a single city study is just that, a single city. Such research can be illuminating and provide the basis for theory building, but there is always the lingering doubt that the findings are somewhat unique to that urban area.

Beyond the decision of case studies versus a national urban sample, research on the performance model of mayoral approval and its racial complications has its own requirements. First, respondents living in cities with African American mayors and African American majorities must be included, and ideally they should constitute about half of the sample in order to maximize the variation on race of the mayor and race of the city which are two of the primary explanatory variables.

Second, in an adequate test of the performance model, the black mayors should not be the first black mayor in their respective city. The high intensity and racial conflict surrounding the first black mayor of any city will inevitably affect the results. Thus, we are seeking cities with *histories* of black mayors in order to reduce the novelty factor of a new minority leader.

Third, the performance model also requires that the mayor be in office long enough to reasonably be held accountable for performance. We do not wish to study a newly elected executive. While there is no conventional number of years after which a mayor, or any executive, comes to be evaluated on performance, we have chosen three years as our threshold. This should be enough time for residents of the city to observe accomplishments, lack of accomplishments, or changes in conditions in the city and begin to hold the mayor responsible.

Fourth, the cities selected must have a history of black/white racial tension. This was accomplished by a review of the racial histories of these cities, and by requiring that each city have at least 20 percent of its adult population of the other race. That is, the majority white cities have at least 20 percent black adults, and the majority black cities have at least 20 percent white adults. It does not make sense to study racial complications to the performance model of mayoral approval in cities with no racial heterogeneity.

Finally, the cities should be located in different regions and have mayors of different parties. Any study that involves race must take into account the difference between the South and the non-South. The unique history of the South with respect to the treatment of blacks, accompanied by the large number of blacks in that region, requires that we examine southern cities as well as non-southern cities. Also, while many mayors are elected in nonpartisan elections, the party of the mayor is still widely known and is a cue for voters to use when deciding whether they approve or not. Thus, there must be some variation in the partisanship of the mayors studied.

Notice that much of the above involves making sure that the researcher selects different types of cities. This is the principle behind the "most different systems" design described in Przeworski and Teune (2001 34–39). The theoretical strength of the most different systems design lies in the potential of finding common patterns of individual behavior across different situations. If individual level relationships are different across the systems, one must resort to systemic explanations. In this research project, the most different systems design means that if we find that the performance model operates in a similar fashion and with similar explanatory power on both black mayors and white mayors, in the South and non-South, and belonging to different parties, there is stronger evidence for the performance model than if the mayors were similar. The most different systems design also allows for system level characteristics, such as the racial composition of the city, to be used as explanatory variables when individual level relationships differ across the cities.

The data for this research are from surveys of black and nonblack (hereafter called "white" for simplicity)[1] registered voters in four cities: Chicago, New Orleans, Detroit, and Charlotte, NC. Two of these cities have black

[1] Self-identified whites dominate the nonblack registered voter samples from each city: 95 percent for New Orleans, 83 percent for Detroit, 91 percent for Charlotte, and 80 percent for Chicago. To test whether the inclusion of Latinos altered the results, we estimated the final Chicago and Detroit models from Chapter 6 including only self-identified whites and blacks. The results were amazingly similar. Details on this analysis are available from the author. This may be because of the screen for registered voters, which obtained the more educated and assimilated Latinos.

majorities and black mayors, Detroit and New Orleans, and the other two cities have white majorities and white mayors, Chicago and Charlotte. Chicago, by far the largest city in the study, contains a substantial Latino population (23 percent).[2] Two are southern cities and two are nonsouthern. One of the white mayors is Republican. All four mayors were in office at least three years at the beginning of data collection, and neither black mayor was the first black mayor in his city.

Studying only four cities inevitably raises the question of generalizability. We make no claim that these cities represent some larger population. We are, however, moving beyond the typical single city approach used in local urban research and differentiating on majority race/race of mayor, party of the mayor, city size, and region. We also set rules for drawing conclusions. We would not accept any finding unless it were true in either three of the four cities, the two majority white cities only, or the two majority black cities only.

A potential problem with the selection of Charlotte and Chicago is that both cities elected a black mayor in the 1980s, possibly producing greater racial tolerance among whites, less alienation among blacks, or greater responsiveness to the black electorate in these cities. These possibilities pose problems for generalizability. However, if our selected majority white cities are more similar to our black cities than other majority white cities we could have chosen, any differences we find due to racial context are more believable.

Another factor to consider is that the two black cities, New Orleans and Detroit, have had black mayors since the 1970s. Having long histories of black mayoral leadership is actually a plus for this research. Given the growth in the proportion of minorities in most urban areas, these cities represent a glimpse into the demographic future. Do citizens eventually evaluate the black mayor using the same calculus that they would for a white mayor? Does approval of black mayors become "normalized" after several generations of black leadership? These questions can best be addressed by studying cities such as New Orleans and Detroit.

Readers might notice the absence of a majority white city with a black mayor and a majority black city with a white mayor. Theoretical and practical reasons drove this decision. First, these situations represent unusual

[2] In spite of the number of Latinos in Chicago, the history of racial conflict in Chicago is overwhelmingly black versus white (Grimshaw 1982; Kleppner 1985). Furthermore, our base random sample of registered voters in Chicago yielded only 8 percent who self-identified as "Hispanic" or "Latino" when asked for their race. This percent of Latino respondents is much smaller than that of the 2000 census figure because: 1) many Latinos do not consider that to be their "race"; 2) the 2000 census asked a separate question about whether or not a person was of Hispanic or Latino "origin," thus identifying Latinos of all races; and 3) Latinos are probably less likely than non-Latinos to be registered to vote.

exceptions, and, given limited resources, we wished to concentrate on the more typical racial patterns. More importantly, we did not want to draw any conclusion based on the findings from one city, so we needed at least two cities with black mayors and black majorities, and two cities with white mayors and white majorities.

An alternative we considered was to use more cities and fewer respondents from each city. The problem was the shortage of black mayors who were either not the first black mayor, or had not been in office three years at the time of site selection. There were plenty of white mayor locations, but far fewer black mayor locations meeting the criteria. So, we settled on a four case-study design. We also avoided the western United States so as not to confound the analysis with histories of Latino/Anglo conflict. This research concentrates on black/white conflict and leaves a Latino study to future research. The percentage of the over 18 population that is black in these cities, according to the 2000 Census, is as follows: Detroit 80.0 percent, New Orleans 62.2 percent, Charlotte 30.1 percent, and Chicago 34.1 percent (United States Census Bureau).[3]

Table 4.1 Race and Latino Ethnic Composition of Adult Populations (18+) of Four Cities (2000 Census)

	New Orleans	*Detroit*	*Charlotte*	*Chicago*
Black	62.2%	80.0%	30.1%	34.1%
White	33.1	14.4	61.4	46.2
Other	4.7	5.6	8.5	19.7
Latino Ethnicity (All Races)	3.3%	4.6%	7.2%	22.8%

This study includes only registered voters living within the city limits whose approval of the mayor is politically influential. Within each city involved in this study, a nearly equal number of black and white registered voters were interviewed. Thus, instead of a cross-sectional representation of each city electorate, we have maximized variation on the key variable of race (King et al. 1994). As a result, we have nearly an equal number of blacks

[3] We should note that the cities were selected and the study was conducted before the 2000 census figures were available. Thus, the cities were selected based on the 1990 census figures. The percent black of the population over 18 in these cities in the 1990 census was Detroit (73 percent), New Orleans (56 percent), Charlotte (29 percent), and Chicago (36 percent).

living with a white mayor in a majority white city as blacks living with a black mayor in a majority black city. It is not the location—Chicago, Detroit, New Orleans or Charlotte—that matters conceptually; it is the race of the mayor and the racial composition of the city that are of concern to this study. Thus, the samples were designed to equally represent cells of a 2 x 2 table of respondent's race and race of the mayor and city. The samples are not designed to be representative cross sections of each city, only representative samples of blacks and of whites within each city.

Cross-sectional, random digit dialing samples of each city's black adults and white adults were utilized, with a screen for registered voters. In order to reach an equal number of minority race respondents (whether white or black) after exhausting the cross sectional sample, we obtained the remaining interviews from areas with a 40 percent or more racial minority concentration. This was necessary due to the practical difficulties and expense of finding respondents from the minority race in a cross-sectional sample. For example, the adult population of Detroit is only 20 percent white, so a cross-sectional sample yielding 250 blacks would include only 112 whites. Adding the more targeted sample to the cross-sectional sample allowed us to obtain the required number of whites without extraordinary costs. However, this method does over-sample minorities (white or black) who live among 40 percent or more of their own race. More detail on the sampling procedure is provided in the Appendix. The final number of respondents by race and by city is presented in Table 4.2.

Table 4.2 Racial Composition of the Sample (Number of respondents)

	New Orleans	*Detroit*	*Charlotte*	*Chicago*
Black	253	282	256	262
White	252	250	273	250

Objective Conditions

At this point it might be helpful to examine a few objective indicators of the quality of life in these four cities. Based on the economic disadvantages of black Americans and previous research on majority black cities, we expect to observe a lower quality of life in the majority black cities (Kraus and Swanstrom 2001). Table 4.3 presents indicators of crime and economic well-being in all four cities.

Table 4.3 Some Indicators of Conditions in the Four Cities

A. Crime

Murders per 100,000 inhabitants	*1999*	*2000*
New Orleans	32.78	41.86
Detroit	43.64	41.61
Charlotte	15.53	13.86
Chicago	22.13	21.79

Violent crime rate per 100,000 inhabitants	*1999*	*2000*
New Orleans	1213	1083
Detroit	2173	2191
Charlotte	1302	1153
Chicago	1911	1631

B. Economy

Percent of population living below poverty level	*1999*	
	Families	*Individuals*
New Orleans	23.7	27.9
Detroit	21.7	26.1
Charlotte	7.8	10.6
Chicago	16.6	19.6

Median Income	*1999*
New Orleans	$27,133
Detroit	$29,526
Charlotte	$46,975
Chicago	$38,625

Median Home Value	*1999*
New Orleans	$87,300
Detroit	$63,600
Charlotte	$134,300
Chicago	$132,400

The statistics on crime present a mixed picture. On one hand, at the time of our research, the murder rate was much higher in the two black cities than in the two majority white cities. In 2000 both Detroit and New Orleans suffered more than forty murders per 100,000 inhabitants. Moreover, the murder rate in New Orleans had clearly increased from the previous year. The majority white cities, Charlotte and Chicago, suffered half or less than half the number of murders per 100,000 than either New Orleans or Detroit. On the other hand, the total violent crime rate, which includes murders and seven other crimes, was not higher in the black cities. In 2000, Detroit had the highest violent crime rate with 2191 per 100,000 inhabitants, followed by Chicago, then Charlotte and New Orleans. And in all cities except Detroit, violent crime had declined compared to the previous year.

We present the murder rate separate from other violent crimes because our research focuses on how citizens perceive conditions in their cities. Murders are the crime that has the most emotional impact on citizens. Murders are described in detail on the nightly news and occupy a central location in the newspapers. Sometimes a local TV network even covers a murder victim's funeral. Murders have devastating effects on families and neighborhoods, and frequently result in crimes of revenge that produce even more fear while eroding trust in neighbors and the police. The other violent crimes, while frightening to the victim and the family, simply do not have the degree or scope of a murder's impact. So, from a citizen's perspective, we expect the higher murder rates in the two black cities to result in lower evaluations of the quality of life.

Economic conditions are also notably poorer in the two black cities. In New Orleans and Detroit approximately one-quarter of the individuals and families lived below the poverty level in 1999. Charlotte was the most prosperous of the four cities with only 7 percent of individuals and 10 percent of families living below poverty, and Chicago fell somewhere in-between with 16 percent of individuals and 19 percent of families below poverty. The story is essentially the same when it comes to median income and median home values. New Orleans and Detroit had the lowest median incomes in 1999 ($27,133 and $29,526, respectively), with Chicago's median income being about $10,000 higher, and Charlotte's median income being another $8,000 higher than Chicago's. Charlotte and Chicago had similar home values, both around $130,000. In contrast, home values were only half of that in Detroit at $63,600 and only $87,300 in New Orleans. The income disparities, along with the proportions living below poverty and the value of homes provide a small glimpse of the economic distance between these majority white cities and majority black cities. By these objective measures, the quality of life is, as we expected, lower in the majority black cities.

Measuring Mayoral Approval and Perceptions of Performance

The dependent variable, *mayoral approval*, is one of the easiest concepts to measure in this entire study. We utilized a simple question that reads, "In general, do you approve or disapprove of the job Mayor (name) is doing?

(pause) Is that strongly or not very strongly?" which produced four response categories ranging from (1) strongly disapprove to (4) strongly approve. This single indicator is similar to the measures used in national and state level studies, and is preferable to something more complicated.

Performance, on the other hand, is the most difficult concept to measure, and we take a more comprehensive approach to measuring performance than national studies that usually rely on one or two performance areas (cf. Edwards et al. 1995; Nadeau et al. 1999). There are many areas which city residents can use to reasonably evaluate local performance. They can have opinions about crime, the local economy, streets, public transportation, traffic control, and a myriad of other municipal services and conditions. City residents can often observe these conditions firsthand and in the course of their daily lives, in contrast to evaluations of national and state conditions, where information and experience are less easy to come by. Furthermore, other than economics, we do not have preconceived notions as to what aspects of performance are most important.

There were twenty-seven individual performance items in the surveys of each city. Dealing with all twenty-seven items would be too unwieldy, so we used principal axis factoring with varimax rotation to get a first look at how the indicators fell into dimensions. Fortunately, there were clear commonalities in the dimensions across the four cities, but not every indicator loaded on the same dimension in every city. We wanted the content of the performance measures to be identical across the four cities in order to make meaningful comparisons; therefore, we did not use factor scores, the content of which differed slightly from city to city. Instead, we used both the results of the factor analysis and the content of the items to place them into scales. The resulting eight dimensions (scales) of performance are described below.

General Evaluations

General evaluations[4] are measured by two questions. A retrospective question asks, "Thinking back over the last five years, would you say that (city name) has become a better or worse place to live, or hasn't there been any change?" The second question is prospective—"And thinking ahead over the next five years, do you think that (city name) will become a better or worse place to live, or won't there be much of a change?" These questions ask for overall impressions of where the city is headed, and they parallel the

[4] Throughout the book, the specific names of variables will have the first letter capitalized.

question at the national level asking whether people think the country is on the wrong track or the right track. Notice that these are not economic evaluations; the respondent can be thinking of any aspects of life in the city when responding. The two questions form reliable additive indices in all four cities with Cronbach's alphas[5] of 0.51 for New Orleans, 0.63 for Detroit, 0.57 for Charlotte, and 0.63 for Chicago.

Economy

Economic evaluations are the performance measure most commonly linked to approval of both presidents and governors. The national- and state-level measures of economic evaluations are typically general, such as inquiries about whether the economy is getting "better," "worse,"or remaining the "same." These are the so-called collective evaluations—people are asked to evaluate the country or state as a whole, regardless of their personal financial situations. Personal financial circumstances are generally regarded as less potent predictors of approval and vote, but some studies have identified a role for personal financial situations (Nadeau and Lewis-Beck 2001; Markus 1992).

At the local level there is probably less psychological distance between collective and personal judgments because the local economy is closer to home. For example, someone experiencing difficulty getting a job is more likely to see the connection between her circumstances and the local employment market than the national employment market. Of course, Americans, as individualists, tend to attribute their personal economic situation to personal events and efforts, but the local economic environment is close, and the connection between personal and local is thus easier to make. Our measure of economic performance includes two collective evaluations and one personal evaluation. The two collective judgments ask residents to rate the following as Very Good, Good, Fair, Poor or Very Poor: "Opportunities for Employment" and "Likelihood of new jobs and industry coming to the city." The personal economic evaluation provides the same responses to "Likelihood of your family increasing its income in the next several years." Additive scales for these three items were computed for each city, and all were reliable, as measured by Cronbach's alpha of 0.68 for New Orleans, 0.72 for Detroit, 0.70 for Charlotte, and 0.74 for Chicago.

[5] Cronbach's alpha is a measure of the reliability or homogeneity of a scale. It ranges from 0.0 to 1.0. The higher the alpha, the more reliable the scale. Typically, alphas of over 0.60 are desirable.

Police

Evaluations of the local Police are one of the three performance dimensions that fall into what might be called a crime and safety category. In most urban areas of the United States, control of crime is a highly salient problem and a logical basis on which to judge the mayor. This is certainly the case in all four cities chosen for this research. When asked an open-ended question about the "biggest problem" facing (city name) today, the most common response was crime. In New Orleans 43 percent mentioned crime, in Detroit 38 percent, in Charlotte 36 percent, and in Chicago 40 percent. No other issue even came close.

There are parallels between crime as an issue at the local level and the economy as an issue at the national level. First, similar to the national media attention paid to the national economy, crime receives a great deal of local media coverage, allowing citizens to judge local government on its ability to control crime. Second, crime, like the economy, has the potential to affect people's lives every day, either by being victimized or by altering one's behavior for fear of crime. Finally, just as in the case of the national economy, someone can have collective judgments about crime in his or her community without ever having been personally a victim of crime. It has even been argued that crime is a functional equivalent at the local level to economic conditions at the national level (Howell and Marshall 1998, 363).

For this study, Police evaluations were measured in all four cities by five items. Respondents were asked to rate each of the following as Very Good, Good, Fair, Poor, or Very Poor: "police protection"; "the ability of the (city name) police to respond quickly to calls for help and assistance"; "the ability of the police to find the criminals after a crime has been committed"; "being courteous, helpful and friendly"; and "avoiding the use of unnecessary or excessive force." We placed the more general "police protection" question in a different section of the questionnaire so that it did not influence the specific items. The additive indices for Police evaluations were quite reliable with Cronbach's alphas of 0.82 for New Orleans, 0.82 for Detroit, 0.81 for Charlotte, and 0.82 for Chicago.

Safety

Safety is the second dimension in the crime and safety category. This performance area is much more personal than evaluations of the police because it involves a citizen's feeling of safety from crime. It is certainly possible to give the police a low rating but still feel personally safe. In fact, it is common for people to give negative responses about general conditions and at the same time be positive about their own personal situation—a pattern which may be characteristic of our optimistic, individualistic American culture (Hochschild 1995; Hibbing and Theiss-Morse 1998).

The Safety performance dimension is measured by three items: "In general, how safe do you feel from crime walking in your neighborhood during the day?"; "During the night?"; and "Walking downtown at night?" with response categories of Very Safe, Safe, Not Very Safe, and Not at all Safe. These three items comprise reliable additive scales with Cronbach's alphas of 0.69 for New Orleans, 0.71 for Detroit, 0.66 for Charlotte and 0.69 for Chicago.

Crime

The final performance dimension in the area of crime/safety is labeled simply Crime. It is a simple question, "Turning to crime and safety, would you say that the amount of crime in (city name) has increased, decreased, or remained about the same over the last several years?" In the exploratory factor analyses, this item did not cluster consistently with the safety items or the police evaluations, so it will be used as a single indicator of citizens' perception about the direction of crime.

Services

In any city there are a myriad of specific city services on which citizens can form opinions. Many of these are quite specific, such as control of litter or quality of parks, and it is doubtful that any one of these services alone would have much impact on mayoral approval. While many citizens might blame the mayor for a rising crime rate, most would not likely blame him for poor litter control—it does not seem as important. However, if evaluations of many city services are combined, the impact could be more substantial. One can imagine a situation where a city is undergoing an economic boom, filling the city coffers, and allowing expenditures on the "little" services to grow. The overall impression a citizen might have is that conditions in the city are improving, and such a generalization could easily translate into approval of the mayor. One can also imagine the opposite situation, a period of decline when many city services are deteriorating or eliminated, leading to a negative overall view and less approval of the mayor.

In this study eight specific city services and one general evaluation of city services clustered into the Services performance dimension. Respondents were asked to rate the following on a scale from Very Good to Very Poor: drainage and flood control, control of abandoned housing, health services, services for the poor, quality of housing, control of litter and trash, parks and recreation, and control of pollution. The final item in this scale asks respondents to rate simply the "overall level of government services." These nine items formed reliable scales in all four cities with Cronbach's alphas of 0.81 for New Orleans, 0.79 for Detroit, 0.76 for Charlotte, and 0.85 for Chicago.

Transportation

Transportation is a critical function in any urban area. In these areas of concentrated population, citizens depend on the government to maintain the streets, provide public transit, and manage traffic. The overall quality of life in urban areas is highly affected by the ability of citizens to get around, and good transportation is an important tool for economic development. This is an area of public policy where even political conservatives prefer more, rather than less, government activity. However, it is an open question as to whether approval of the mayor is affected by the quality of transportation.

Our measure of performance in Transportation consists of three items which respondents were asked to rate as Very Good, Good, Fair, Poor or Very Poor: "conditions of your local streets and roads"; "availability of public transportation within the city"; and "control of traffic congestion." The additive scales from these items are reliable as indicated by Cronbach's alphas of 0.53 for New Orleans, 0.57 for Detroit, 0.49 for Charlotte, and 0.63 for Chicago.

Schools

Public schools may seem like an odd performance measure to include in a model of mayoral approval. However, two of our cities, Chicago and Detroit, have shifted from elected to mayoral-appointed school boards (Wong and Shen 2003), giving the mayor a key leadership role in school reform. In addition, the quality of public schools, or lack thereof, often receives a great deal of media attention, and schools become a point of either pride or embarrassment for a community. Therefore, they become a yardstick by which citizens judge the quality of life in their city whether or not they have any personal experience with the schools.

Our measure of citizen evaluations of the public Schools is one simple, five-category item rating the public schools in their city from Very Good to Very Poor. As we might expect, this item did not empirically fit with the other performance dimensions, so it will be used as a single item measure.

In sum, eight scales covering a wide range of topics measure perceptions of performance: General Evaluations, Services, Police, Safety, Economy, Crime, Transportation and Schools. The range of topics is designed to make the point that, conceptually, the local level is more than just the third level below the national and state level. The meaning of local "performance" is qualitatively different in that citizens can and will use more of their own experiences and observations in making local performance judgments. In contrast, most information about state and national conditions is obtained from the media or other secondhand sources. This distinction gives "performance" at the local level a richness and complexity that is not possible at the two higher levels of government.

Measuring Conditions in the Neighborhood

Research indicates that both objective neighborhood conditions and individual characteristics such as race and income influence how urban residents perceive conditions in their cities. To estimate the effects of race alone on performance evaluations we must control for some measure of neighborhood conditions. There are no geographic locator variables in these data. The only measure available is a question about neighborhood racial composition "How would you describe your neighborhood racially—almost all white, mostly white, about an equal number of blacks and whites, mostly black, or almost all black?" This question is not exactly objective, but it is often the case that conditions in homogeneous black neighborhoods are less desirable than in homogeneous white neighborhoods.

Measuring Racial Attitudes

The racial attitudes of both blacks and whites are crucial concepts in our performance model of mayoral approval. Whites' and blacks' racial attitudes are expected to affect mayoral approval both directly and indirectly through influencing the performance measures. These concepts have proven fruitful in numerous studies, but there is tremendous variation in the actual measures utilized, and, in addition, there is some intellectual debate as to the value of some of these measures. So selecting measures of white racial attitudes and black racial attitudes is not an easy task.

Black Racial Attitudes

The crucial racial attitude for blacks is some form of black consciousness. One form of black consciousness is labeled "common fate" or "linked fate"—the notion that blacks recognize that they are often treated categorically in spite of interpersonal differences, and, therefore, what happens to blacks generally has implications for each individual. Linked Fate is measured by Michael Dawson's question: "Do you think what happens generally to black people in this country will have something to do with what happens in your life?" (if yes) "Will it affect you a lot, some, or not very much?" (Dawson 1994).

As mentioned in Chapter 1, there can be a behavioral component to black consciousness, which we have called Black Solidarity. This component involves black unity in political, social and other matters to achieve objectives that benefit blacks. The four items we use to measure Black Solidarity are taken from one or more of the National Black Election Studies: "How important is it for blacks to vote for black candidates when they run for office—extremely important, very important, or only somewhat important?" (not very important could be volunteered); "How important is it for blacks to participate in black-only organizations whenever possible?"; "How important is it for blacks to have control over the government in mostly black communities?"; and "How important is it for blacks to have control over the economy in mostly black communities?"

Two of these items are explicitly behavioral: voting and belonging to black organizations. The other two items have to do with the balance of power in black communities: asserting that, if the population is mostly black, then blacks should be in control of the government and economy. These items are directly relevant to our two majority black cities, where we expect Black Solidarity to be positively related to both the performance scales and to mayoral approval. That is, the more solidarity a black citizen believes in, the more pride he or she will have in the majority black city and the black mayor. All four items were combined into additive scales which were reliable in all four cities: 0.79 for New Orleans, 0.80 for Detroit, 0.77 for Charlotte, and 0.75 for Chicago.

White Racial Attitudes

There is more controversy about how to best conceptualize white racial attitudes than black racial attitudes due to a lack of consensus over a definition of racism and the emotionally charged nature of that word. Is racism the old belief in black inferiority? Does it mean belief in stereotypes? Is it a rejection of black culture? Or fear that blacks represent a threat to white dominance? All of these have been suggested by scholars as the basis for current antiblack attitudes among whites.

This research utilizes two concepts, Symbolic Racism and Group Conflict, in the models of mayoral approval among whites in four cities. The first, Symbolic Racism, also called "racial resentment," has been useful in predicting racial policy views and voting behavior when black candidates are involved. Symbolic Racism is defined as a blend of antiblack feelings with a racialized form of individualism (Sears 1988; Kinder and Mendelberg 2000). It is a belief among whites that most blacks do not live up to the American work ethic, and that they receive undeserved preferential treatment. Symbolic Racism has received considerable support from studies of elections that involve Tom Bradley in Los Angeles (Kinder and

Sears 1981; McConahay and Hough 1976; Sears and Kinder 1971) and as a predictor of racial policy views (Sears et al. 1997; Bobo 2000). All of these studies show an impact of Symbolic Racism over and above standard influential variables such as ideology and party identification.

A second approach to white racial attitudes, Group Conflict, is the notion that whites' racial attitudes are based upon their sense of group position and their feelings of entitlement to social resources, status, and privileges. Thus, whites' resentment of blacks is due to blacks being competitors for privileges and resources (Bobo and Hutchings 1996; Blumer 1958). Like Symbolic Racism, Group Conflict has been used to predict opinions on racial policies even when controlling for other political attitudes (Bobo 1998, 2000). It seems reasonable that the notion of competition for resources would be quite relevant in an urban setting where racial groups often "compete" for neighborhoods, public sector jobs, and elective offices. As we have argued, racially diverse cities are settings where racial attitudes, among both whites and blacks, are primed nearly every day, and the closeness of the other group cannot help but lead to feelings of competition.

Symbolic Racism is measured by four items selected due to their inclusion in the 1986 through 1994 American National Election Studies.

"Over the past few years blacks have gotten less than they deserve."

"Irish, Italians, Jews and other minorities overcame prejudice and worked their way up. Blacks should do the same without any special favors."

"In past studies, we have asked people why they think white people seem to get more of the good things in life in America—such as better jobs and more money—than black people do. These are some of the reasons given by both blacks and whites. It's really just a matter of some people not trying hard enough. If blacks would only try harder they could be just as well off as whites."

"Generations of slavery and discrimination have created conditions that make it difficult for blacks to work their way out of the lower class."

All items were answered on a five-point scale from Strongly Agree to Strongly Disagree, and the reliability of the additive scales in each city is: 0.55 for New Orleans, 0.46 for Detroit, 0.57 for Charlotte, and 0.60 for Chicago.

The Group Conflict items clearly tap perceptions of competition between blacks and whites:

"More good jobs for blacks means fewer good jobs for members of other groups."

"The more influence blacks have in local politics, the less influence members of other groups will have in politics."

"As more good housing and neighborhoods go to blacks, the fewer good houses and neighborhoods there will be for members of other groups."
"Many blacks have been trying to get ahead at the expense of other groups."

Again, the items were scored from Strongly Agree to Strongly Disagree and the reliability coefficients are: 0.83 for New Orleans, 0.74 for Detroit, 0.78 for Charlotte, and 0.82 for Chicago.

Race and Mayoral Approval

Before testing components of the model, we will take an initial look at how whites and blacks in these cities view their mayors. Mayoral approval is racially polarized in all four cities, but not always in the expected direction (Table 4.4).

Table 4.4 Mayor Approval by Race (standardized residuals in parentheses)

		White	*Black*
New Orleans	Strongly Disapprove	25% (3.1)	8% (-3.1)
(Black City)	Disapprove	13% (1.3)	8% (-1.3)
	Approve	36% (1.1)	28% (-1.1)
	Strongly Approve	26% (-3.6)	56% (3.6)
	Pearson's r = 0.31***	100%	100%
		N = 235	N = 238
Detroit	Strongly Disapprove	13% (-2.1)	24% (2)
(Black City)	Disapprove	6% (-2.0)	14% (1.9)
	Approve	36% (0.2)	35% (-0.2)
	Strongly Approve	45% (2.5)	27% (-2.3)
	Pearson's r = -0.22***	100%	100%
		N = 237	N = 266
Charlotte	Strongly Disapprove	4% (-2.1)	11% (2.3)
(White City)	Disapprove	3% (-2)	10% (2.2)
	Approve	40% (-0.1)	41% (0.2)
	Strongly Approve	53% (1.7)	38% (-1.9)
	Pearson's r = -0.22***	100%	100%
		N = 253	N = 216
Chicago	Strongly Disapprove	6% (-1.9)	14% (1.9)
(White City)	Disapprove	7% (-1.6)	13% (1.6)
	Approve	30% (-0.4)	33% (0.4)
	Strongly Approve	57% (2)	40% (-1.9)
	Pearson's r = -0.20***	100%	100%
		(243)	(250)

Note: *** $p < 0.001$.

In three of the cities, New Orleans, Charlotte, and Chicago, the predictable pattern exists, with whites more likely to approve of the white mayor, and blacks more likely to approve of the black mayor. However, in Detroit, former Mayor Dennis Archer, an African American, was more popular among whites than among blacks. This reverse polarization in Detroit is an anomaly we will return to shortly.

There are some striking similarities in racial polarization across these cities. The *difference* in overall mayoral approval between whites and blacks ranges from a low of 14 percent in Chicago to a high of 22 percent in New Orleans, indicating that the differences between whites and blacks are substantial and not dramatically different in magnitude across the four cities. The similarity in racial polarization is further illustrated by the bivariate correlations between being black and approval of the mayor: -0.20 in Chicago, -0.22 in Charlotte, -0.22 in Detroit, and 0.31 in New Orleans.

In all four cities, the difference between whites and blacks is strongest in the categories of "strongly approve" and "strongly disapprove," indicating that intensity of support, as well as direction, is affected by race. The "strongly approve" category is where racial polarization is particularly apparent; in this category the *difference* between whites and blacks ranges from 15 to 30 percent. In contrast, the difference between whites and blacks in the "approve" category ranges from only 1 percent to 8 percent. It may be an easy thing to say "approve" in answer to a question about how you think the mayor is handling his job, but to say "strongly approve" requires a sincerity and certainty that the simple "approve" answer does not. The large standardized residuals in the "strongly approve" cells also confirm racial polarization in intensity. Larger standardized residuals in a cell indicate a greater difference between the observed and expected values for that cell. So, the significant racial polarization in the percentage of respondents who "strongly approve" of these mayors is probably a better indicator of racial effects than the overall approval levels.

Reverse racial polarization in Detroit presents an interesting and theoretically important exception to the generalization that citizens are more likely to approve of mayors of their race than mayors not of their race. While a majority of both whites and blacks approved of Archer, his approval rating was higher among whites. This case is theoretically important because it demonstrates that racial polarization can exist even in the reverse direction due to the persistence of different racial agendas. Mayor Archer disappointed black voters on several fronts. For one, he did not take a strong stand against welfare reform, which was supported by Michigan's Republican governor. Some observers criticized Archer, saying that the economic revitalization of the city benefited whites much more than blacks (Farley, et al. 2000). Furthermore, he simply was not Coleman

Young, the charismatic leader of the civil rights movement in Detroit, and the first African American mayor in that city—a position he held for twenty years. Mayor Archer's style was more technocratic and legalistic. The reverse racial polarization in Detroit confirms other analyses suggesting that personal style has implications for the mayor's relationships with white and black constituents (Perry 2000, 1990). Thus, for both instrumental and symbolic reasons, Mayor Archer was more popular among whites than blacks.

All of the evidence above is preliminary and bivariate, but it provides an initial indication that performance models of mayoral approval should include race as an explanatory factor. Our model predicts that opinions on performance are also racially polarized; blacks and whites will view certain city services and aspects of the quality of life differently. Specifically, our expectation, as expressed in Hypothesis Three, is that

> Blacks are more negative than whites about evaluations of performance, and the difference is accentuated in majority white cities.

To take an initial look at racial differences in opinions on performance, we have correlated race with eight specific performance dimensions in all four cities (Table 4.5).

Table 4.5 Racial Polarization on Performance Dimensions. Pearson Correlations. Race X Dimension

Performance Dimension	*New Orleans*	*Detroit*	*Charlotte*	*Chicago*
General Evaluations	0.03	0.05	0.04	-0.27***
Police	-0.14**	-0.03	-0.32***	-0.29***
Services	-0.005	-0.06	-0.15**	-0.26***
Safety	-0.07	0.18***	-0.24***	-0.18***
Economy	-0.02	-0.004	-0.28***	-0.22***
Transportation	-0.02	-0.11*	0.10*	-0.13**
Crime Decreasing	-0.01	-0.01	-0.13**	-0.22***
Schools	0.29***	0.07[a]	0.11**	0.04

[a] $p < 0.10$
* $p < 0.05$
** $p < 0.01$
*** $p < 0.001$

Higher correlations mean that there are greater differences in black and white perceptions of performance in that area, Two conclusions can be drawn from the pattern of correlations in Table 4.5. First, consistent with our expectations, the racial polarization on performance dimensions is much more prevalent in majority white cities than the majority black cities. Of the sixteen relationships between race and performance, fourteen reach standard levels of statistical significance[6] in the majority white cities, while only four reach that level in the majority black cities. Thus, the difference in how whites and blacks view conditions in their cities is greater in the majority white cities.

Particularly interesting are the differences between black and white perceptions of the Police and the Economy. These are the areas where we expect to observe the greatest differences between blacks and whites. We expect racial polarization in police evaluations because of the historically conflicting relationship between blacks and police, and we expect it in economic outlook, due to the stark socioeconomic differences between blacks and whites. The racial differences are larger in the majority white cities; in Charlotte and Chicago blacks give less positive evaluations of the Police and are less optimistic about the Economy than whites. However, in the majority black cities of New Orleans and Detroit, there is no consistent pattern of lower black evaluations in these performance areas.

City Services are a third area where we might expect differences in blacks' and whites' evaluations because blacks, who are disproportionately low income, must rely on these services more than whites. In City Services evaluations a pattern similar to Police evaluations and the Economy emerges; blacks are more negative than whites in the majority white cities, but there are no racial differences in the majority black cities.

Blacks and whites also have different views of the trends in Crime in the majority white cities, but not in the majority black cities. In Charlotte and Chicago, black residents are less likely than whites to say that crime is declining. This certainly makes sense when considering that blacks in majority white cities are more likely to live in isolated high crime areas. In contrast, in majority black cities black residents are scattered geographically, with some living in areas plagued by high crime and some living in safe

[6] Statistical significance is simply a probability that the result from the sample actually reflects the full population within a certain margin of error, or confidence level. For example, a significance level of 0.05 means that there is only a 5 percent chance that the actual population value does not fall within the confidence interval around the observed value. Those not familiar with statistical significance need only know that the lower the significance level, the better. That is, 0.001 represents a higher level of statistical significance than 0.05.

neighborhoods. The result is that while blacks have more experience with crime than whites in all cities across America, the difference in blacks' and whites' experience with crime is accentuated in majority white settings where blacks are more likely to be geographically isolated. In the majority black cities there are no racial differences in opinions as to whether Crime is decreasing or increasing.

There is racial polarization on the Safety dimension as well but with a slightly different twist. As in the case of perceptions of Crime trends, blacks are predictably less likely to feel safe than whites, and this is only the case in the majority white cities. However, black residents in Detroit actually feel safer than whites do, a reversal of the relationship in the majority white cities. This may be the effect of whites being a small minority. Whites make up only 20 percent of the over-eighteen population of Detroit, and tend to live in very isolated, small enclaves (Danziger and Farley 2000). Even though they are economically advantaged, due to their small numbers, they may feel overwhelmed and somewhat helpless when faced with a large black majority, thereby making them less likely to respond that they feel safe. The white population of New Orleans is a more robust 37 percent, and, compared to Detroit, their neighborhoods are larger, producing a greater sense of safety.

One of the patterns we observed is that, overall, blacks do not have more positive evaluations than whites of conditions in the cities where they are in the majority. Majority black cities have been labeled "empowerment zones," and some studies have shown blacks to have higher levels of political trust, efficacy, and participation than whites in settings where blacks are in the majority (Bobo and Gilliam 1990; Howell and Fagan 1988). The attitudes and behaviors studied by Lawrence Bobo and Franklin Gilliam are all political and civic orientations, which are logically affected by which race is in political power. However, the more positive outlook of blacks in civic affairs does not extend to a more positive outlook on the quality of life. Examining the New Orleans and Detroit columns of Table 4.5, eleven of the sixteen correlations between race and the performance dimensions are not even statistically significant, meaning that black and white evaluations are essentially the same. In only two cases are black evaluations more negative than white evaluations, and three relationships are in the opposite direction. So, the overall conclusion from this initial bivariate analysis is that blacks are similar to whites across the board about the quality of life in the majority black cities. However, in the majority white cities, blacks do give more negative evaluations than whites on most performance dimensions.

Although these are only bivariate tests, social dominance theory and the group competition model support their findings. In the majority white cities, the normal group hierarchy exists, with whites in the dominant position. In these contexts it is to be expected that blacks will have less positive evaluations of conditions in their cities than whites. In contrast, in the majority black cities, the harsh conditions are a countervailing force to the psychic boost blacks get from seeing members of their own race in political power. On top of that, whites are alienated in the majority black cities by being in the unusual subordinate position and by the objective conditions. The net result is less racial polarization in perceptions of performance in the majority black cities.

Another way of illustrating the different reactions of whites and blacks to the racial composition of their cities is to separately examine, for whites and for blacks, simple bivariate relationships between living in a majority black city and the performance dimensions. Table 4.6 presents correlations between living in a majority black city and the performance dimensions.

Table 4.6 Racial Composition of City and Performance Dimensions. Pearson Correlations. Black City X Dimension

Performance Dimensions	*Among Blacks*	*Among Whites*
General Evaluations	0.08*	-0.08*
Police	-0.11***	-0.31***
Services	-0.32***	-0.46***
Safety	0.00	-0.27***
Economy	-0.23*** -	0.43***
Transportation	-0.26***	-0.22***
Crime Decreasing	0.21***	0.07*
Schools	-0.23***	-0.34***

[a] $p < 0.10$
* $p < 0.05$
** $p < 0.01$
*** $p < 0.001$

Negative correlations mean that living in a majority black city is associated with lower performance evaluations. A black environment has more negative consequences for whites' perceptions than for blacks' perceptions; all but one of the correlations among whites are significant and negative, and for six of the eight performance dimensions, the negativity of the relationship is greater for whites than for blacks. Thus, the preliminary evidence is as predicted—a black environment has more consequences for whites than for blacks.

A few graphs illustrate these patterns with simple percentages (Figure 4.1).

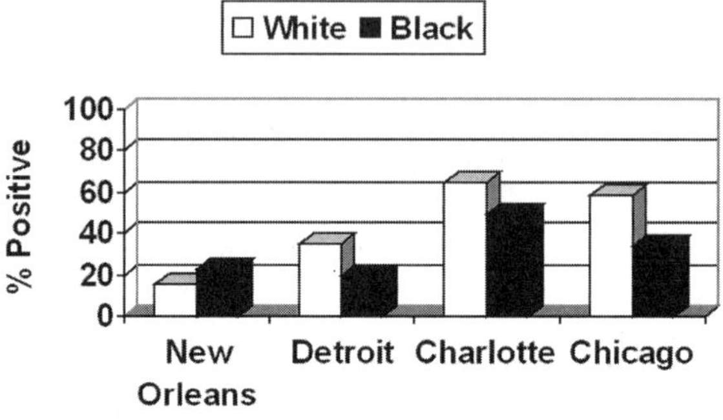
Overall Government Services
White
Black
100
80
60
40
20
0
% Positive
New Orleans
Detroit
Charlotte
Chicago

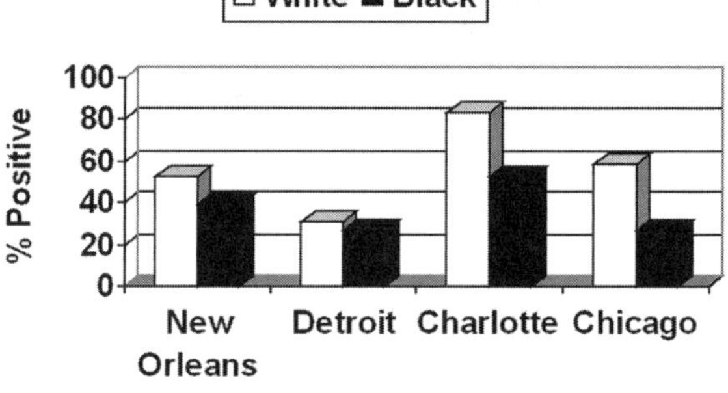
Quality of Police
White
Black
100
80
60
40
20
0
% Positive
New Orleans
Detroit
Charlotte
Chicago

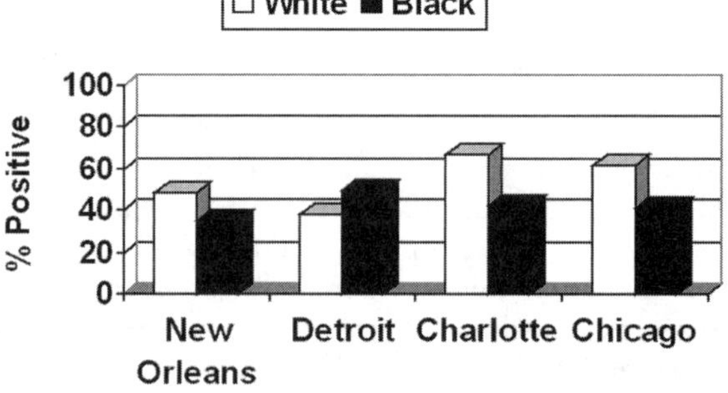
Safety at Night
White
Black
100
80
60
40
20
0
% Positive
New Orleans
Detroit
Charlotte
Chicago

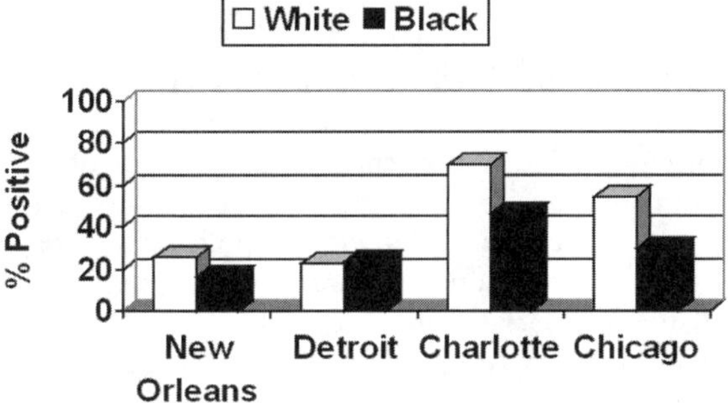

Employment Opportunities

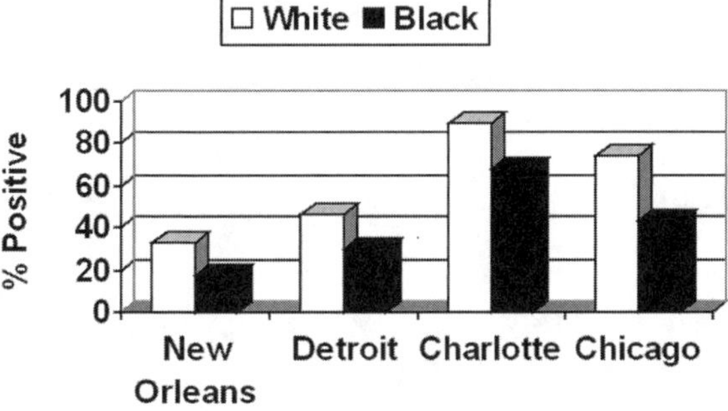

Figure 4.1 Selected Performance Items by Race and City

The items in the graphs are some of the single indicators that are contained within the multi-item scales. The height of the bars indicates the percent who rate the item positively. It is obvious that the difference between whites and blacks is greater in the majority white cities than in the majority black cities. Also, whites are more positive in the majority white cities than in the majority black cites, whereas the difference among blacks is less pronounced and less consistent.

In sum, based on the preliminary bivariate analysis, race is significant in a performance model of mayoral approval in these cities. There is the predictable racial polarization in mayoral approval, and there is also racial polarization in the majority white cities on perceptions of performance. It also seems that the racial composition of the city affects these relationships.

However, social scientists should never be satisfied with bivariate findings. The racial polarization on performance could be a function of socioeconomic status, not race itself. Lower income people could have more negative perceptions of conditions in the city simply because of their personal circumstances. Racial differences in perceptions of the city could also be due to conditions in black neighborhoods. Or, racial polarization in mayoral approval could be a function of political ideology; blacks are more liberal than whites. Multivariate analysis is necessary to say with some confidence that race or racial context is actually having the effects suggested by the bivariate findings. Also, we have not yet examined the racial attitudes, which are expected to affect both the performance dimensions and mayoral approval. The next two chapters estimate multivariate models of the eight performance dimensions and mayoral approval, models that include a series of control variables. As we will see, the role of race and racial context remains.

Chapter 5
How Race Affects Performance Evaluations

The role of race in a performance model of mayoral approval is not limited to its direct impact on approval of the mayor. As we have mentioned, race may be antecedent to the standard performance model and may affect citizens' perceptions of conditions in the city, as illustrated by path b in the model in Chapter 1. This is reasonable to expect because blacks and whites occupy opposite positions of privilege in our society, and, given these positions, we predict that blacks will view conditions in their environments more negatively than whites. In addition, we expect this greater black negativity to be especially pronounced in the majority white cities because blacks are in the minority position, both economically and politically. In contrast, in the majority black cities, the psychological boost of political advantage will lessen blacks' negativity about conditions in the city and thereby reduce the differences between blacks and whites. To restate Hypothesis Three:

> Blacks are more negative than whites about evaluations of performance, and the difference is accentuated in majority white cities.

A preliminary look at racial differences in evaluations of performance in the last chapter yielded some interesting results. In the majority black cities the most common pattern across the eight performance dimensions is that blacks and whites have similar perceptions. In only a few cases are blacks more negative than whites as predicted by the hypothesis, and in a few instances blacks are even more positive. However, the situation is quite different in the majority white cities. Racial polarization's effect on performance is much more prevalent in the majority white cities, and the pattern was exactly as predicted—greater black negativity. In Charlotte and Chicago blacks hold more negative attitudes than whites toward the Police, their Safety, the Economy, city Services, and the direction of Crime in the city.

Before we accept the conclusion that blacks are more negative than whites, but only in the majority white cities where they are the minority, we must control for some obvious variables. Are blacks more negative than whites because they are of lower economic status? Are blacks more negative than whites because they receive a lower quality of services in their neighborhoods or they have a greater need for services in their neighborhoods? Are whites more positive than blacks about the performance dimensions because they are more politically conservative and thereby expect less of government? These questions are crucial because this research is about *race*, and the sociopsychological identification it implies. It is not about economic status, neighborhood differences, or political ideology and how they influence perceptions of life in the city. We must isolate the unique effects of race itself on the performance measures in order to have some confidence that the racial polarization we observed in the bivariate analysis is not due to other factors.

In order to estimate the unique effects of race we have added six variables to multivariate models of each performance dimension. Multiple regression estimates the effects of each independent variable on the dependent variable while controlling for other independent variables. For example, if race still has an effect on evaluations of the Police while controlling for the other variables, we have more confidence that race itself is indeed affecting Police evaluations. On the other hand, if race is no longer statistically significant when controlling for the six variables, then one or more of those variables accounts for the bivariate racial differences that we have already observed, and we cannot say that race as self classification has any effect.

The six control variables are income, education, living in a black neighborhood, age, gender, ideology, and race of interviewer. All are plausible influences on perceptions of performance. Among these controls, the most obvious influences on evaluations of conditions in the city are income and education—both indicators of socioeconomic status—and living in a black neighborhood. The higher the status of a person, the more likely he or she will be to live in a better neighborhood, associate with other high status people, and thus have less contact with the negative aspects of their city. Living in a black neighborhood is expected to be associated with lower performance evaluations due to poorer conditions in most homogeneous black neighborhoods and possibly a lower quality of municipal services (Van Ryzin et al. 2004). Gender and age are both expected to be associated with perceptions of safety since females and older people typically feel more threatened by crime. Older people are also more likely to have positive attitudes toward the police, since they rely on the police for their protection. It is less easy to explain how ideology might influence perceptions of the quality of life except to say that white conservatives might be more negative about the quality of life in majority black cities and more positive in majority white cities. Regardless of the effects of ideology, we want to be confident that the racial differences observed in performance evaluations are due to race, not political ideology. The race of the interviewer is included because responses of blacks and white often differ depending on whether they think the interviewer is black or white (Davis and Silver 1999; Finkel et al. 1999).

Race and Performance Evaluations—Multivariate Analysis

Separate city multivariate results are presented in Table 5.1A in accordance with the most different systems design. This approach requires examining the cities separately to see if the same individual level relationships hold across the systems. The effects of race are not consistent across the cities. When we control for the seven other factors, race only affects a few dimensions in more than one city, and these are mostly in the majority white cities.

To simplify the presentation, Table 5.1A includes only the coefficients representing the effects of race, living in a black neighborhood, and the overall fit for the regression models; coefficients for other control variables are not presented in order to keep the table simpler. We present the statistically significant coefficients only so that readers can easily isolate what is important. Our first conclusion is that the effects of race are concentrated on evaluations of city Services, perceptions of the Police, and evaluations of public Schools, and the effects of race on Services and Police evaluations are only found in the majority white cities. In Charlotte and Chicago, blacks have more negative opinions than whites of the Police and city Services, but in the two majority black cities, race has no effect on either of these two performance areas. In the case of public School evaluations, blacks are more positive about the public Schools than whites, but there is no racial pattern to the cities where this occurs. Other than these three areas, there are only sporadic racial effects on performance.

To be confident that racial polarization is higher on the dimensions of Services and Police in the majority black cities, we tested for interactions of race X black city in Table 5.1B. If this term is statistically significant, it means that the white city/black city differences in racial polarization are probably real and not due to chance. Both of the interaction terms in Table 5.1B are highly significant, meaning that the impact of race on Police and city Services evaluations differs depending on the racial majority of the city.

The second conclusion is that whites' attitudes about the Police and city Services are more affected by the racial composition of the city than blacks' attitudes. That is, while both whites' and blacks' opinions about conditions in the city are, as expected, more negative in the majority black cities, the

Table 5.1 Race and Dimensions of Performance

A. Dependent Variable	*New Orleans (Black city)*			*Detroit (Black city)*			*Charlotte (White city)*			*Chicago (White city)*		
	Race (Black)	Black Neighborhood	R^2	Race (Black)	Black Neighborhood	R^2	Race (Black)	Black Neighborhood	R^2	Race (Black)	Black Neighborhood	R^2
OLS												
Services	—	—	—	—	—	—	-0.03[a]	—	.02	-0.06**	-0.07*	0.11
Police	—	-0.09*	0.06	—	—	—	-0.08***	—	0.14	-0.10***	-0.08*	0.15
Safety	—	-0.13*	0.06	0.11***	—	0.09	—	-0.13**	0.19	—	-0.12*	0.09
Economy	—	-0.15***	0.02	—	—	—	-0.07**	—	0.21	—	-0.17***	0.21
Transportation	—	-0.07[c]	0.04	-0.05*	—	0.02	—	—	—	—	-0.08*	0.03
OLOGIT[b]			BIC' [c]			BIC'			BIC'			BIC'
General Evaluations	—	—	—	—	—	—	—	—	—	-0.63*	-0.89*	-0.85
Crime Decreasing	—	—	—	—	—	—	—	—	—	—	-0.90*	3.68
Schools	1.09***	—	-7.85	—	—	—	0.43[a]	—	21.02	—	—	—

B. Pooled Model [d]	*Race (Black)*	*Age*	*Education*	*Conservative Ideology*	*Black Neighborhood*	*Black City*	*Race * Black City*	R^2	*N*
OLS									
Services	-0.05***	—	—	—	-0.05***	-0.16***	0.05***	0.20	1694
Police	-0.09***	0.02***	0.01**	0.02**	-0.09***	-0.13***	0.09***	0.14	1724

Table 5.1 Race and Dimensions of Performance *continued*

Note: [a] $p < 0.06$, * $p < 0.05$, ** $p < 0.01$, *** $p < 0.001$. for the OLS models cell entries are unstandardized regression coefficients for the race and black neighborhood variables and the adjusted R^2's. In Part A cells with dashes indicate an insignificant regression model based on the F statistic or insignificant relationships between Race and Black Neighborhood and the dependent variable. Race is coded is a dichotomous variable; 0 = nonblack, 1 = black. Black neighborhood is coded from 0, meaning all white, to 1 meaning all black. All models in Part A include controls for gender, income, education, age, ideology, and race of interviewer, but coefficients are not presented for the sake of brevity.

[b] Ordered logit is the appropriate estimation technique when the dependent variable is ordinal and has fewer than six categories. Under these circumstances many of the assumptions of OLS are violated, making the coefficients inefficient (Long 1997). Cell entries for ologit cannot be interpreted as regression coefficients and are quite difficult to interpret without computing predicted probabilities or graphing. Since, in this analysis, there are no patterns worth describing, predicted probabilities are not computed and simple significance is noted. Dashes indicate an insignificant ologit model based on the probability of Chi-square or an insignificant relationship between Race and Black Neighborhood and the dependent variable.

[c] The best goodness of fit measure for ordered logit is the BIC' value (Bayesian Information Criterion), which assesses whether the model fits the data sufficiently well to justify the number of parameters that are used (Long 1997). All of the ologit models where data are presented in the table are significant models as measured by the Chi-square probability. However, in two cases the BIC' value is positive, meaning that the model is very poor given the number of explanatory variables. The BIC' puts a very high value on parsimony and a positive BIC' probably means that there are too many variables in the model. However, we wanted to show the impact of race in the presence of the same controls that we are using throughout this research.

[d] The models in Part B contain all the same controls as the separate city models. Controls that are insignificant in both the Police and Service Models are not presented.

difference is greater for whites. The specific numbers that support this are in Table 5.1B. The column titled "Black City" is the impact a black majority environment has among whites. These numbers can be interpreted as follows: whites rate Services 16 percent lower and the Police 13 percent lower in the majority black cities than in the majority white cities regardless of their economic status, age, political ideology, race of their neighborhood, and the other control variables. The comparable figures for blacks are 11 percent and 4 percent. In the last chapter we observed this white "sensitivity" to the racial environment without any controls for other factors. Now we can see that, when it comes to the Police and municipal Services, living in a majority black city affects whites more than blacks regardless of many other factors.

What is beginning to emerge is a tentative conclusion that white evaluations of two important quality of life dimensions differ more than black evaluations in response to the racial environment. As we have argued before, a white majority is the normal environment in America, one in which whites hold the political and economic balance of power. As the dominant group, whites are able to define what the normal racial, social and political order is. In fact, whites often do not have a sense of racial consciousness or ethnicity simply because they do not need it in an environment so suited to their interests (Gallagher 2003; Chesler et al. 2003). Sociologists have called this the "invisibility" of whiteness because white is perceived as natural (Chesler et al. 2003). This is the environment to which most whites and blacks are accustomed.

When whites find themselves in the unusual position of being the minority group, the reaction is predictably negative. The negativity is expressed in opinions about aspects of urban life, and it is exacerbated by the typically depressed conditions in majority black cities. Blacks, on the other hand, do not have a parallel "boost" in their evaluations of performance when they are in the majority, possibly because it is counterbalanced by those same depressed objective conditions.

The white/black difference in opinions about city Services is graphically displayed in Figure 5.1, which shows the predicted values on the Services scale for blacks and whites depending on whether they live in a majority black or majority white city, while holding all of the control variables constant at their means. Change from a white environment to a black environment means a decline in Services evaluations for both black and white residents, but the slope of the decline is slightly greater for whites.

The relevance of these statistics to the model of mayoral approval is that if there are racial differences on evaluations of city Services in the majority white cities only, even if they are small, and if we ultimately find that

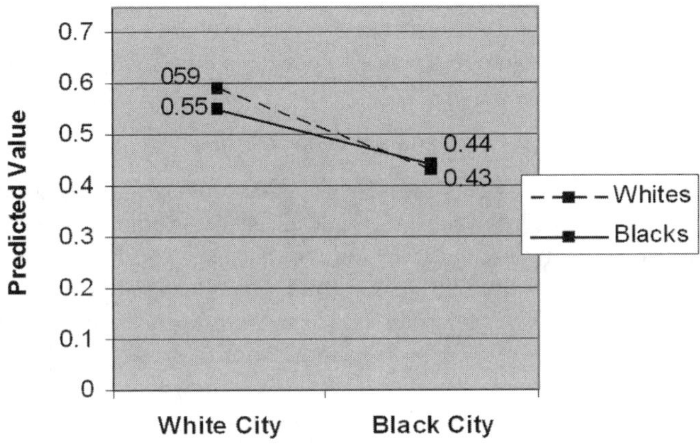

Figure 5.1 City Services

Services evaluations influence who approves or disapproves of the mayor in these cities, then race indirectly affects mayoral approval.

At this point I should point out a comprehensive study of fifty-two municipalities that produced results seemingly contradictory to ours. Melissa Marschall and Anirudh Ruhil (2005) found that black mayors have a positive effect on blacks' perceptions of neighborhood conditions. Our two studies can be reconciled by a close look at the cities under investigation. Marschall and Ruhil focus on the presence of a black mayor whether or not there is a black majority population. Five of the ten black mayors in their study do not govern majority black cities. It is possible that under black leadership blacks have more positive perceptions than under white leadership, but only up to the point where the poverty of most majority black cities overtakes the positive effect of having a black mayor.[1]

The final conclusion from Table 5.1 is that living in a black neighborhood has a negative impact on perceptions of performance in several instances; the more homogeneously black the neighborhood, the more negative the perceptions, particularly of Safety and the Economy. Because

[1] Marschall (2005) also researched 197 school districts and found that having blacks on the school board resulted in higher evaluations of the schools among blacks. The vast majority of these districts were not majority black, which may account for the inconsistency between Marschall's findings and the findings here.

blacks are more likely to live in segregated neighborhoods (Scott 2001), controlling for this variable gives us more assurance that the effects of race on the citywide perceptions are not due to poor neighborhood environments.[2]

Race and Police Evaluations

In this section we take a closer look at the effects of race and the racial environment on evaluations of the Police due to the historically racialized nature of that urban institution. It is well known that blacks and whites hold different views of the police (cf. Decker 1981; Campbell and Schuman 1968; Smith et al. 1991). The underpinnings of these differences are both historical and current, having their basis in the role of the police in maintaining social order and in the position of blacks as a minority group. Historically, the relationship between blacks and the police has been problematic, fluctuating from being mildly strained to openly confrontational. For more than half of the twentieth century, the police enforced Jim Crow laws in the South, and they did so in ways that ranged from being disrespectful to being brutally oppressive. Current issues involve police brutality, racial profiling, and generally more aggressive policing of blacks and their neighborhoods. Furthermore, the crime problem in the United States has become racially charged due to higher crime rates in minority neighborhoods, exaggerated media portrayals (Entman 1992a 1992b; Peffley et al. 1996), and the political rhetoric of politicians who talk about crime in racially coded language (Edsall and Edsall 1991; Jamieson 1992; Mendelberg 2001). Given all of this, racial differences in attitudes toward the police are predictable.

Many studies have demonstrated that blacks have greater animosity than whites toward the police. A report produced by the U.S. Department of Justice, Bureau of Justice Statistics found that, while overall satisfaction with law enforcement is high, black Americans are twice as likely as white Americans to be dissatisfied with the police in major metropolitan areas (Greenfield et al. 1997). More recently, another Bureau of Justice Statistics national survey confirmed the results of the earlier study and reported that, while the police enjoy a generally favorable image among the public, racial differences continue to exist. Specifically, blacks are less likely than whites to express a favorable opinion of the police, to have confidence in the police, or to think the police should use force in any situation (Bureau of Justice Statistics 2000). Finally, in studies of both the Los Angeles area and

[2] "Black neighborhood" is not a purely objective measure of neighborhood conditions. It has a psychological component as well as an objective component. That is, blacks and whites may feel gains or losses of status depending on the race of their neighborhood. These feelings are also being measured by the race of neighborhood variable.

the Detroit area, wide interracial gulfs were found in perceptions of the extent of racism and discrimination among the city's police (Tuch and Weitzer 1997; Sigelman et al. 1997; Welch et al. 2001). Even on matters regarding the efficiency with which the police provide their services to communities, African Americans hold less favorable views than whites. On the issue of response time, which is universally regarded to be an important standard measure of the efficiency of police service, blacks express a higher level of dissatisfaction with police than whites (Bloch 1974, 22–25, Furstenberg and Wellford 1973, 393–406, Fogelson 1968, 217–247).

In our two majority white cities, race has more impact on evaluations of Police than on any other performance dimension.[3] The coefficients in Table 5.1A can be interpreted to say that, controlling for neighborhood racial composition, income, education, gender, age, ideology and race of interviewer, blacks rate the Police 8 percent lower in Charlotte and 10 percent lower in Chicago. Again, the racial differences are not large in an absolute sense, but they are more impressive when you consider that the effects of other important variables are being accounted for.

Racial differences in Police evaluations can be put to an even stronger test. Perceptions of crime and experiences with crime are additional criteria by which citizens may evaluate the police. We will call these "crime-based" factors as a way to distinguish them from racial factors. The first crime-based factor is victimization. It is well established that blacks are more likely to be crime victims than whites. In fact, blacks have the highest rate of violent victimization of any other racial group (National Center for Victims of Crime 2004). They are also more likely to be the victims of property crimes, especially household burglary, than whites or other racial groups (Bureau of Justice Statistics 2003). Maybe blacks have lower evaluations of Police because they are so often the victims of crime.

The second crime-based factor is less personal. It is simply the respondent's perceptions about the trend in crime in the city—whether it is getting worse, staying the same, or improving. These perceptions are a result of media reports, personal experiences, or both, as when personal experiences are enhanced by what is seen in the media (Mutz 1994). A belief that crime is increasing or decreasing is translated easily into lower or higher opinions of the police.

[3] Two ordered logit coefficients (ordered logit is explained briefly in Table 5.1, Footnote b), one in Charlotte and one in Chicago, are numerically larger than the regression coefficients in the models of Police. Since ordered logit coefficients cannot be directly compared to regression coefficients, we computed predicted probabilities of the most positive Police evaluation for blacks and for whites in both cities, holding all control variables at their means. The impact of race on Police evaluations is larger in both cities.

In order to isolate the unique effects of race, our model of Police evaluations must include measures of the crime-based factors. The measures available in the survey are:

whether the respondent or anyone in the household had been victim of crime in the past three years
whether the respondent thinks crime in the city is increasing, decreasing, or remaining the same

Table 5.2A presents the effects of these crime-based factors and race on evaluations of Police in our four cities.

Table 5.2 Race and Police Evaluations

A. OLS Regression Models[b]		*Y = Police Evaluations*		
	New Orleans	Detroit	Charlotte	Chicago
Race (Black)	—	—	-0.09***	0.10***
Black Neighborhood	—	—	—	—
Crime Decreasing	0.10***	0.10***	—	0.08**
Victimization	-0.08***	-0.07***	-0.07***	-0.06**
Adj. R^2	0.14	0.10	0.18	0.19
N	421	434	442	427

B. Pooled Model[c]	*Y = Police Evaluations*
Race (Black)	-0.09***
Black City	-0.13***
Race X Black City	0.08***
Black Neighborhood	-0.07***
Victim	-0.08***
Crime Decreasing	0.05***
Age	0.02***
Education	0.01*
Conservative Ideology	0.02*
Adj R^2	0.19
N	1724

Note: [a] $p < 0.10$, * $p < 0.05$ ** $p < 0.01$ *** $p < 0.001$

[b] All models in Part A contain controls for gender, income, education, age, ideology, and race of interviewer. Cell entries are unstandardized regression coefficients.

[c] The model in Part B contains the same control variables as the separate city models. However, only the significant variables are presented.

The crime-based factors have predictable effects. In three cities, citizens who believe crime is decreasing are more positive about the Police, and in all four cities victimization is negatively related to opinions about the Police. In addition, the impact of each of these crime factors is remarkably similar across the cities. Believing that crime is decreasing is associated with an 8–10 percent increase in Police evaluations, and being a victim results in a 6–8 percent decline, taking into account race, race of neighborhood, and the demographics.

However, the crucial question for our purposes is whether race still affects evaluations of Police when controlling for these crime factors. The answer is yes, but only in the majority white cities. This is basically the same conclusion we reached without the crime factors; whites and blacks have similar opinions about the Police in the majority black cities, but blacks are less positive than whites about the Police in the majority white cities. The particular coefficients in Table 5.2A can be interpreted to mean that blacks are 9 percent lower on the Police evaluations scale than whites in Charlotte and 10 percent lower in Chicago, regardless of the racial composition of their neighborhood, whether they think crime is increasing or decreasing, whether they have been victimized, socioeconomic status, and other characteristics. Race also adds explanatory power. Notice that the coefficients of determination (Adj. R^2) are higher in the majority white cities, 0.18 and 0.19 in Charlotte and Chicago compared with 0.14 and 0.10 in New Orleans and Detroit.

Racial Context and Police Evaluations

Prior to adding the crime-based factors to the models of Police evaluations we tentatively concluded that the greater racial polarization in the majority white cities is due to the fact that whites, not blacks, are more affected by their racial environment. When we take into account the crime-based factors, the same conclusion is supported. In Table 5.2B we have pooled the data from all four cities while adding an interaction term for race X black city. The coefficient for Black City, -0.13, is interpreted as the impact among whites of living in a majority black city. That is, whites in the majority black cities are 13 percent lower on the Police evaluations scale than they are in the majority white cities. This figure is exactly the same as it was without the controls for crime perceptions and victimization (Table 5.1B). Among blacks, the effect of living in a majority black city on evaluations of the police is less, -0.05 (computed as -.013 + 0.08).

The white/black difference in reaction to the racial environment is graphically displayed in Figure 5.2, which shows the predicted scores on the Police evaluation scale depending on type of city while holding all control variables, including the crime-based factors, constant at their means.

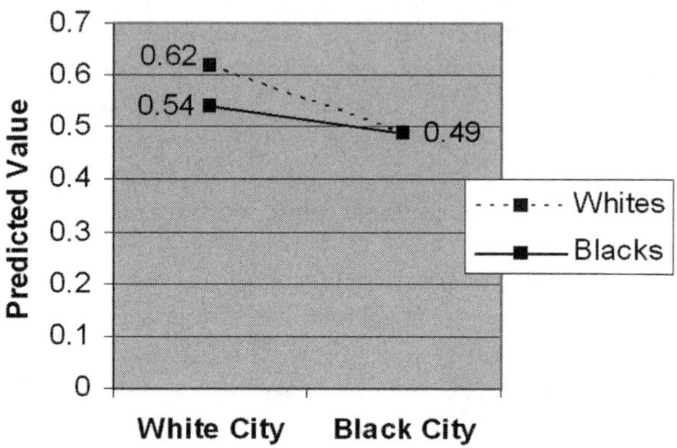

Figure 5.2 Police Evaluations

The change from a white environment to a black environment means a decline in Police evaluations for both whites and blacks, but the slope of the decline is greater for whites. The greater white reaction to living in a majority black environment exists regardless of an impressive list of other factors that might explain it.

In sum, Hypothesis Three is partially confirmed in the case of Police evaluations. Blacks are no more negative than whites in the two majority black cities, but they are definitely more negative than whites in the two majority white cities, even when controlling for numerous other factors.

As in the case of city Services, this model of Police evaluations is relevant to the ultimate goal of explaining approval of the mayor. If racial polarization on evaluations of Police exists only in the majority white cities, and if we find that Police evaluations influence who approves and who disapproves of the mayor in these cities, then race will be indirectly affecting mayoral approval.

This principle applies to any racial differences observed in Table 5.1A. For example, in New Orleans blacks rate the public Schools significantly higher than whites do. If the citizens of New Orleans judge the mayor partly on their perceptions of the public Schools, race will have played a part in those perceptions. Our point is that racial differences may take several paths on their way to influencing opinions of the mayor.

Racial Context and the Other Performance Dimensions

Racial context not only affects evaluations of Police and city Services. It also affects both blacks' and whites' attitudes toward five of the other six performance measures: feeling of Safety, perceptions of the Economy, Transportation, and public Schools (Table 5.3).[4]

Table 5.3 Racial Context and Remaining Performance Dimensions (full models in Appendix Table A.3)

Dependent Variable *N=1724*	*Black City*	R^2
OLS		
Safety	-0.05***	0.10
Economy	-0.14***	0.20
Transportation	-0.09***	0.07
OLOGIT		BIC'
Crime Decreasing[a]	0.56**	-54.02
General Evaluations	—	30.25
Schools	-1.26***	-184.65

Note: * p < 0.05, ** p < 0.01, *** p < 0.001.

[a] The finding that respondents are more optimistic about crime in the black cities is only due to the negative responses in the city of Charlotte. The other white city, Chicago, is similar to New Orleans and Detroit. Thus, we will not draw conclusions based on this finding. See Table 5.4.

As expected, public evaluations of most of these aspects of the quality of life are lower in the two majority black cities than in the two majority white cities, regardless of whether or not one lives in a black neighborhood. Most obvious are the effects of racial context on citizens' opinions of the public Schools, which can best be understood in terms of probabilities. In the majority white cities the probability of rating the public Schools as Poor or Very Poor is only 0.24, but in the majority black cities the probability of such poor ratings is 0.54.[5] Less dramatic, but still negative, are the differences from majority white cities to majority black cities in public

[4] According to our rules for drawing conclusions, we cannot make statements about the differences between "white cities" and "black cities" unless the pattern holds for both white cities or both black cities. The purpose of this rule is to prevent us from drawing conclusions based on only one city. All of the conclusions in this section were tested by reestimating the model while dropping one city at a time. Except for the findings about Crime Decreasing, the impact of racial context was essentially unchanged.

[5] These predicted probabilities were computed while holding all other variables at their means.

perceptions of the Economy, Transportation, and Safety. All of this is consistent with the objective conditions faced by citizens, black and white, in these majority black cities.[6]

Contrary to conventional expectations, the trend in Crime is not perceived as worse in the majority black cities. Given the crime problems that typically plague cities where blacks are the majority, we would have predicted that citizens in those cities would be more pessimistic about the Crime trend in their locales. However, a look at responses to the Crime question across the four cities reveals why perceptions of Crime are not affected by the racial composition of the city (Table 5.4A). In New Orleans, Detroit, and Chicago about one-third of respondents say crime is decreasing, but Charlotte stands out in stark contrast with only 13 percent of blacks and 17 percent of whites believing that crime is decreasing.

Perceptions do not necessarily reflect reality. The actual trend in total violent crime was downward in Charlotte, so why would so few residents say, "crime is decreasing"? The answer lies in the dramatic increase in murders that occurred in Charlotte between 1997 and 1999 (Table 5.4B). Over these two years the murder rate increased by 50 percent. Even though Charlotte had the lowest murder rate of any of the four cities, Charlotte stands out as the only city among the four experiencing an increase in murders; all of the other cities experienced a decline in the murder rate over the same time period. In particular, the two majority black cities had instituted aggressive police reform programs in the mid-1990's which were given credit for reducing crime, and especially reducing murders, in those cities (Smockl 1999). As we argued earlier, murders have a tremendous emotional impact on citizens due to their prominence on the nightly news and the devastating effects on families and neighborhoods. From a citizen's perspective, higher murder rates are more threatening and attention getting than increases in most other violent crimes. Thus, it is reasonable that respondents in Charlotte react to the higher murder rates by responding that "crime is increasing" in their city.

The Crime measure may be one of the weakest performance measures in our study. Respondents are simply asked whether they think crime has increased, decreased, or remained about the same over the past year. This is a question about a trend. Nearly all of the other questions ask about conditions right at that time. So it is possible for someone to say that crime is

[6] In the pooled models, Black Neighborhood also has a largely negative impact on the quality of life dimensions, but in the individual city models (Table 5.1) Black Neighborhood only affects feelings of Safety in three of the four cities. So, given our rules for drawing conclusions, we can only say with confidence that living in a Black Neighborhood reduces feeling of Safety.

Table 5.4 Perceptions of Crime in the Four Cities

A. Perceptions	*New Orleans*		*Detroit*		*Charlotte*		*Chicago*	
Crime has:	Black	White	Black	White	Black	White	Black	White
"Increased"	34%	31%	26%	24%	60%	45%	38%	19%
"Stayed the Same"	31	35	37	39	27	38	35	39
"Decreased"	35	34	37	37	13	17	27	42
N	253	252	282	250	256	273	262	250

B. Murder Rates (per 100,000)	*New Orleans*	*Detroit*	*Charlotte*	*Chicago*
1997	54.88	49.30	10.90	26.28
1998	47.45	45.20	12.02	24.31
1999	32.78	43.64	15.53	22.13
2000	41.86	41.61	13.86	21.79

increasing, and at the same time believe that the situation is not yet very bad, or it is possible to believe that the crime situation is stable and at the same time believe that crime is very threatening. For this reason we think that the Police and Safety questions are better measures of citizen evaluations of crime conditions than the single indicator about the direction of crime.

Finally, there is no impact of city racial context on General Evaluations. Recall that General Evaluations are measured by two questions about whether the city "as a place to live" has gotten better, worse, or stayed the same over the last five years and whether the respondent expects the city to get better, worse, or stay the same over the next five years. There are two potential problems with these questions. First, like the crime question, respondents are asked about a trend, not about conditions at that particular time. So, again, someone may think conditions are poor, but also believe that there has been no change. The second problem with these general opinions is that they may be affected by mayoral approval. That is, people who approve of the mayor may generalize their approval to global evaluations of where the city is going, and those who disapprove of the mayor may be more pessimistic about the direction of the city. This will be a problem when using General Evaluations as a predictor of mayoral approval because there may be causation in both directions. The issue of mutual causation will be dealt with in the next chapter.

At this point, given the complexity of the findings, a summary is in order. Hypothesis Three, that

> blacks are more negative than whites about evaluations of performance, and the difference is accentuated in majority white cities,

is largely disconfirmed. In the two majority black cities, blacks and whites have similar perceptions of nearly all of the performance areas. Also, in these cities blacks are more positive than whites when evaluating public Schools. However, Hypothesis Three has some support in two crucial areas—city Services and the Police. Black residents are less satisfied than whites in these two areas and only in the majority white cities. The racial differences in opinion about Services and the Police in the majority white cities are not large in an absolute sense, but they are more impressive when you realize that they survive controls for powerful factors such as racial composition of the respondent's neighborhood, socioeconomic status, ideology, age, gender, and crime-based variables.[7]

[7] The crime-based factors are only included in the model of Police evaluations, not the models of city Services.

In addition, living in a majority black city has a negative effect on both whites and blacks. Both racial groups have lower opinions of six of the eight aspects of performance if they live in one of the majority black cities, a pattern that is probably predictable given the actual conditions in the two majority black cities. However, it is the whites who exhibit the greatest *reaction* to the racial environment. When it comes to city Services and the Police, whites' evaluations decline more than blacks' evaluations when the environment changes from white to black.

How Racial Attitudes Affect Performance Evaluations

Race itself is not the only racial factor that influences how people evaluate performance in racially diverse settings. Racial *attitudes* also affect how people view conditions in their environment. Neither blacks nor whites are homogeneous in their views on racial matters. Within each race there are variations in racial consciousness and variations in animosity toward the other race. These variations can be expected to affect how an individual reacts to racial stimuli, such as the racial composition of the environment or the race of the people in political power.

The racial attitudes of both blacks and whites are related to theoretical foundations in social dominance theory and the group competition model. The dominant group develops its own "ideology" that supports its position, and the subordinate group develops another ideology that both explains its position and offers ways to overcome it. The racial attitudes of blacks and whites, such as black consciousness and white racism, are expressions of those ideologies.

White Racial Attitudes and Performance Evaluations

Most whites in America live in situations where they are the undisputed majority. They may encounter minorities at work and about town, but racial issues are largely symbolic and without relevance for their everyday lives. Our four cities cities are a different situation. In these cities racial attitudes are primed by both everyday life and by the local media. As we argued earlier, it is almost impossible not to think about one's views about racial matters in settings of racial diversity.

Even more unique for whites are situations in which they are not the majority. We predict that racial attitudes will be particularly influential when whites are in the unexpected position of being the minority race because anxiety and hostility will activate their racial attitudes. Given whites' loss of status, it is reasonable to expect them to perceive that conditions in the city are changing for the worse, an expectation that is, unfortunately, often reinforced by an actual decline in city conditions. This entire process is expected to be more pronounced among whites who possess the most antiblack racial attitudes. Thus Hypothesis Five is that

> in a majority black context, whites with conservative racial attitudes will be more negative about the quality of life in their city than whites with liberal racial attitudes. A reverse relationship is expected in majority white contexts.

Testing this hypothesis means separating out whites and estimating the influence of their racial attitudes on the eight performance dimensions in each of the four cities. Two racial attitudes are utilized in the models. The first is Symbolic Racism, which is defined as a combination of antiblack feeling with a belief that blacks do not live up to the American work ethic ideals. This is a socially acceptable way of denigrating blacks through the perception that they fall short when it comes to traditional American values such as individualism and self-discipline. The second white racial attitude is Group Conflict, the belief that gains by blacks are at the expense of whites. This is a more tangible, less theoretical, racial attitude than Symbolic Racism. It refers to whites' fear of losing the material goods and social and political influence they have become accustomed to. This fear can be expected to increase when blacks gain in numbers, and particularly when they gain political dominance.

Overall, and contrary to Hypothesis Five, whites' racial attitudes do not have much influence over performance evaluations (Table 5.5). However, as hypothesized, the impact of white racial attitudes is felt more in the majority black cities. Of the thirty-two coefficients in the majority black cities, eight reach standard levels of statistical significance, while in the majority white cities only one of the thirty-two coefficients reaches significance. Most significant effects are in the expected direction—whites with higher levels of Symbolic Racism or a higher sense of competition and conflict with blacks have lower evaluations of performance. However, with one exception, the pattern of white racial attitude effects is sporadic, appearing here and there across the cities and dimensions.

The one exception is a familiar one. White racial attitudes have their most consistent impact on evaluations of Police in the majority black cities. In both New Orleans and Detroit where the police forces are majority black, whites with a greater sense of competition with blacks give the Police lower evaluations. The magnitude of the racial attitude effects is quite strong. Movement from perceiving the least competition with blacks to the most is associated with a change of 24 percent and 17 percent down the scale of Police evaluations. In contrast, in the majority white cities, the effects of white racial attitudes on Police evaluations are nonexistent.

Table 5.5 Racial Attitudes and Dimensions of Performance among Whites

A. Dependent Variable[b] *OLS*	*New Orleans (Black city)*			*Detroit (Black city)*		
	Symbolic Racism	Group Conflict	R^2	Symbolic Racism	Group Conflict	R^2
Services	—	—	—	—	—	—
Police	—	-0.24***	0.12	—	-0.17**	0.11
Safety	-0.19*	—	0.07	—	—	—
Economy	—	-0.19**	0.12	—	—	—
Transportation	—	—	—	—	—	—
OLOGIT			BIC'			BIC'
General Evaluations	—	—	—	-1.74*	-1.15*	29.79
Crime Decreasing	-1.82*[c]	-1.55**	11.63	—	—	—
Schools	—	—	—	—	—	—

B. Pooled Model[d] *OLS*	*Y = Police Evaluations*
Black City	-0.09***
Group Conflict	-0.08[a]
Group Conflict*Black City	0.09[a]
Black Neighborhood	-0.06*
Victimization	-0.06***
Crime Decreasing	0.05**
Age	0.02***
Education	0.01*
Conservative Ideology	0.03**
R^2	0.22
N	799

Note: Only one of thirty-two coefficients associated with white racial attitudes was significant in the white cities. Therefore, the results are omitted for the sake of brevity.

[a] $p < 0.10$, * $p < 0.05$, ** $p < 0.01$, *** $p < 0.001$.

[b] All models in Part A include controls for gender, income, education, age, ideology, black neighborhood, and race of interviewer, but coefficients are not presented for the sake of brevity. Cell entries are unstandardized regression coefficients.

[c] Explanation of ologit coefficients and the BIC' is in the footnotes to Table 5.1.

[d] The model in Part B contains the same control variables as the separate city models. However, only the significant variables are presented. Cell entries are unstandardized regression coefficients.

Here is more evidence of the racialized nature of opinions of the police, only this time, we are seeing within-race racialization. We have already observed that whites view the Police more negatively if they live in a majority black city, and now we see that, within those majority black cities, whites with more antiblack attitudes are even more negative about the Police.

White racial attitudes retain their influence on Police evaluations in the two majority black cities even when controls are added for perceptions of the crime trend and victimization (data not shown in Table 5.5). When these two variables are added to the police models in Table 5.5, the coefficient for Group Conflict only drops from -0.24 to -0.20 in New Orleans and from -0.17 to -0.16 in Detroit, both relatively small decreases. Taking into account these two additional factors—perceptions of the crime trend and victimization—it is even more convincing that whites with conservative racial attitudes are more negative toward the Police in majority black cities.

The greater impact of white feelings of Group Conflict on evaluations of the Police in majority black cities is supported when the data from all four cities are pooled (Table 5.5B). The interaction between Group Conflict and living in a majority black city is negative and approaches significance with a p value of 0.08. In plain English this means that living in a majority black city increases the impact of whites' feelings of Group Conflict on Police evaluations, and we can be fairly confident that the difference between the majority white cities and the majority black cities is not due to chance.

It is probably best to see the interaction in a graph (Figure 5.3).

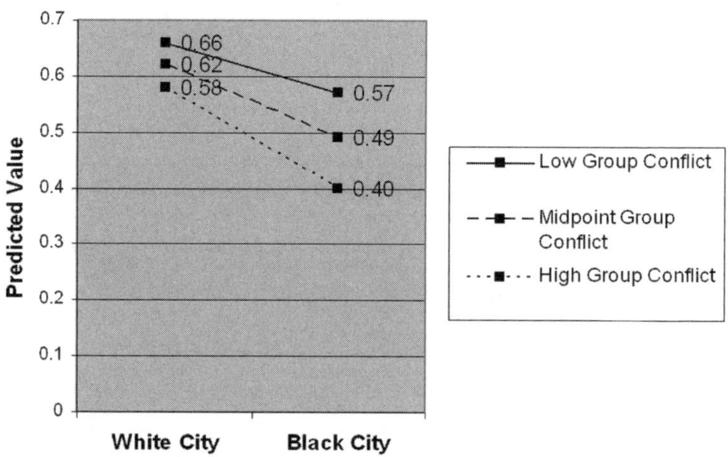

Figure 5.3 Police Evaluations and White Racial Attitudes

The three lines represent three levels of feelings of Group Conflict with blacks, the lowest (0), the middle of the scale (0.5), and the highest (1.0). One can readily see that the three lines are further apart in the majority black cities than the majority white cities. In the majority black cities, whites with a low sense of conflict with blacks give the police a 0.57 rating on the Police scale, while whites with a high sense of competition with blacks give police a 0.40 rating. This computes to a 0.17 difference depending on a white person's racial attitude. On the other hand, in the majority white cities, that difference is only half of that amount, 0.08, computed as 0.66 minus 0.58.

It is interesting, and theoretically important, that Group Conflict, not Symbolic Racism, is the crucial racial attitude affecting white evaluations of Police in the majority black cities. Recall that Group Conflict is the notion that gains made by blacks are at the expense of whites. Thus, it has a more direct connection than Symbolic Racism to the larger social dominance approach that we are taking in this research. Simply put, dominant groups regard gains on the part of subordinate groups as a direct threat, and situations in which blacks have both numerical dominance and political power will activate group competition or conflict on the part of whites. In the case of the Police, whites' "losses" in the majority black cities may be their sense of order and safety in a majority black world.

Supporting this argument, the sense of Group Conflict is indeed higher among whites in the majority black cities than in the majority white cities (Table 5.6).

Table 5.6 Correlations between Being in a Black City and Having Antiblack Attitudes on the Group Conflict Scale (whites only)

	Correlation
All White Respondents	0.14***
Without New Orleans	0.08*
Without Detroit	0.18***
Without Charlotte	0.06[a]
Without Chicago	0.20***

[a] $p < 0.10$
* $p < 0.05$
** $p < 0.01$
*** $p < 0.001$

Among all white respondents, the correlation between living in a majority black city and feeling a high sense of Group Conflict with blacks is 0.14 (p<.001). In keeping with our own rules for drawing conclusions, we have to be sure that one city is not producing the relationship. So, one by one the cities are dropped from the computation. Still the positive relationship between living in a majority black city and feeling a greater sense of competition with blacks remains, meaning that no single city is responsible for the pattern. There is no similar correlation between living in a majority black city and having a high score on Symbolic Racism.

Black Racial Attitudes and Performance Dimensions

We also expect black residents' racial attitudes to affect the way blacks view conditions in these racially diverse cities. The key racial attitude among blacks is black consciousness—the awareness that historical and current disadvantages bind blacks together and carry implications for unified action. Higher levels of black consciousness should be associated with positive evaluations of conditions in the majority black cities due to the pride and psychological lift from having members of their race in positions of power. The opposite is expected to occur in majority white cities. Due to their economic and political disadvantage, blacks with higher levels of racial consciousness should be less positive about conditions in majority white cities than blacks with lower levels of racial consciousness. These expectations are formally expressed as Hypothesis Seven:

> In a majority black context, black consciousness is positively related to evaluations of performance. A reverse relationship is expected in majority white contexts.

Michael Dawson's notion of "linked fate" and the notion of black solidarity represent black consciousness. Linked fate is the belief that one's own life chances are linked to those of blacks as a group (Dawson 1994). Black solidarity is the notion that blacks need to join together in social, educational, and political endeavors in order to protect their interests. Black solidarity means that blacks should belong to organizations to benefit blacks, vote for black candidates, patronize black businesses, and engage in other behaviors that support the black community.

The results indicate that neither linked fate nor black solidarity have any pattern of effects on perceptions of conditions in the cities (Table 5.7). Blacks with high levels of black consciousness are not more positive in the majority black cities, nor are they more negative in the majority white cities. There are a few significant coefficients, but we cannot base statements on only one majority black city or one majority white city. Thus, we have no evidence for a systematic role for black racial attitudes as determinants of the performance dimensions.

Why, with the exception of white Group Conflict and the Police evaluations, are racial attitudes so weak when compared to race itself in affecting

Table 5.7 Racial Attitudes and Dimensions of Performance among Blacks

A. Dependent Variable	*New Orleans (Black city)*			*Detroit (Black city)*		
	Linked Fate	Black Solidarity	R^2	Linked Fate	Black Solidarity	R^2
OLS						
Services	—	—	—	—	—	—
Police	-0.06*	-0.11*	0.09	—	—	—
Safety	-0.09*	—	0.08	—	—	—
Economy	—	—	—	—	—	—
Transportation	—	—	—	—	—	—
OLOGIT			BIC'			BIC'
General Evaluations	—	—	—	—	1.53	31.59
Crime Decreasing	—	-1.18*	13.20	—	—	27.18
Schools	—	—	—	—	—	—

B. Dependent Variable	*Charlotte (White city)*			*Chicago (White city)*		
	Linked Fate	Black Solidarity	R^2	Linked Fate	Group Conflict	R^2
OLS						
Services	—	—	—	—	—	—
Police	-0.07*	—	0.05	-0.06	—	0.04
Safety	—	—	—	—	—	—
Economy	—	—	—	—	—	—
Transportation	—	—	—	—	—	—
OLOGIT			BIC'			BIC'
General Evaluations	—	—	—	—	—	—
Crime Decreasing	-0.77*[b]	—	23.55	—	—	—
Schools	-0.69*	1.26*	23.31	—	—	—

Note: [a] p < 0.06, * p < 0.05, ** p < 0.01, *** p < 0.001. All models include controls for gender, income, education, age, ideology, black neighborhood, and race of interviewer, but coefficients are not presented for the sake of brevity.

[b] Explanation of these coefficients and the BIC' is in the footnotes to Table 5.1.

how citizens view conditions in their cities? The explanation may lie in the powerful nature of racial identification. Simply being black or white, stripped of any overlay of racial attitudes, is enough to produce different perspectives across a wide variety of topics. In cities with histories of racial division such as these, the within race differences pale in the face of the ever-present racial identity represented by the simple demographic—race.

Summary

In this chapter we examined differences between whites' and blacks' views of conditions in their cities under the assumption that race would play an antecedent role in the performance model of mayoral approval. For most of the performance dimensions, in all four cities, race does not play such a role; black and white perceptions are similar when controlling for socioeconomic status and the racial composition of the neighborhood. However, the exceptions are important ones. Evaluations of city Services and the Police, and the influence of race on these performance items is apparent in the majority white cities.

It is important to note that the effects of race on Services and the Police are not large in an absolute sense; the black/white differences range from 0.03 to 0.10. However, these racial differences exist independent of race of neighborhood, socioeconomic status, political ideology, gender, age, and the race of the interviewer, which are controlled for in all models.

So what do these racial differences mean? By using controls for the obvious explanations, we have tried to isolate the effects of race alone, as a self-classification. But we could not empirically explain away all racial differences with information in the surveys. The racial differences in perceptions of performance could be due to actual differences in the realities experienced by blacks and whites, untapped by race of neighborhood, differential socialization, or both. Disentangling these factors is beyond the scope of this book. What is important is that perceptions are interpretations of each person's reality, and blacks and whites interpret the reality of conditions in the majority white cities differently when it comes to the quality of Services and the Police. Ultimately, this may affect their view of the political leadership, specifically the mayor.

Using multiple dimensions of performance at the local level is more useful than deciding *a priori* that any particular dimension is the most important, or trying to summarize all performance areas in general questions. In fact, our general performance dimension, General Evaluations, did not display any racial polarization at all, nor could it be explained by a collection of the standard demographics. The concept "performance" at the local level is both complex and personal. Citizens, their families, and their friends observe performance in many areas of their daily lives. Blacks and whites also bring their differing racial perspectives to some areas of performance and not to others. Therefore, it is much more instructive to conceive of performance as consisting of multiple dimensions.

Two racial context measures, living in a black neighborhood and living in a majority black city, both influence how citizens perceive conditions, usually with negative implications. Consistent with the plight of many blacks in urban areas, a black neighborhood and a majority black city each make their own unique contribution to a pessimistic view of city conditions. These contextual variables have both objective and subjective components. Objectively, conditions are worse in most black contexts than white contexts, and subjectively, whites and blacks may judge both their neighborhood and their city partly on its racial composition. We are most concerned with the effects of the race of the city because that is the electorate for the mayor, but we have controlled for the racial composition of respondent's neighborhood because it can also affect perceptions of the city.

Contrary to what was predicted, on most performance measures, whites and blacks seem equally affected by whether they live in a majority black or majority white city. However, when it comes to city Services and the Police, whites "react" more than blacks to a predominantly black environment. We have argued that this white reaction is due a violation of the normal environment in America in which whites hold the political and economic balance of power. Furthermore, it is interesting that the white reaction to a black environment is greater on the Police dimension than on any other performance dimension. Police are the keepers of order in society and historically have been one of the instruments of white control. So it should be no surprise that when whites are in the unusual situation of being in a black environment with black police, their evaluations of those police decline the most.

On the whole, neither white racial attitudes nor black racial attitudes have much influence over perceptions of conditions in these cities. The one exception is that whites' sense of group competition with blacks is associated with lower evaluations of the Police in the majority black cities, and the effect is substantial. That is, whites who feel that blacks' gains are their losses are more negative about the Police than whites who do not feel that way. Again, police are representatives of the black regime.

In sum, the performance dimensions are perceptions of various aspects of life in the city, and most of them are not affected by race when controlling for other key factors. However, there are two crucial exceptions where blacks and whites bring their own racial perspectives to bear on observations about performance. The racial environment of the city is a more powerful influence on performance perceptions, particularly among whites, who are sensitive to finding themselves in the minority. So, when we estimated the effect of performance on mayoral approval, we have already included racial factors in the background.

Chapter 6

Explaining Mayoral Approval

Mayors arguably have more influence over the quality of urban citizens' daily lives than any other executive in our political system. They influence policies that are "close to the ground" such as funding for police, streets, public housing, zoning, transportation, and economic development. Although they are certainly constricted by city councils and state and federal regulations, mayors still have the ultimate executive power in their cities. Yet, despite the potential impact of mayors on the quality of life in urban areas, the connection of citizens to their mayors via approval has not often been studied using systematic scientific methods.

Studies of presidential and gubernatorial approval have been based on a performance model, meaning that citizens evaluate conditions in the state or the nation and judge the president or governor accordingly. In state and national studies economics have been the most prominent explanatory factor in the approval models. We have argued that performance at the local level, while having an economic component, also contains a number of other dimensions, such as crime control, the quality of streets, public transportation, parks, traffic, and schools. Furthermore, many of aspects of urban life can be observed up close in the course of daily life, in contrast to conditions in the state or the nation. Urban residents can, therefore, judge mayoral performance firsthand; whereas they must rely for the most part on the media when assessing conditions in their state or the nation. Thus, when it comes to mayors, performance has a complex and personal nature not possible at the national or state level.

The major complication in applying the performance model to mayors is the role of race. The increasing number of African American mayors, and the racial diversity of many urban areas, require that race and racial factors be included in an explanation of why people approve or disapprove of the mayor. Three racial factors are incorporated into the model of mayoral approval: race as a simple self-classification, the racial attitudes of whites and blacks, and the racial composition of the city. How much is mayoral approval in these cities influenced by race and racial attitudes, and how much is mayoral approval influenced by citizen evaluations of conditions in the city, i.e., performance? Are certain aspects of performance more important for mayoral approval than others? Is the relative influence of race and racial attitudes vs. performance different for white mayors compared to black mayors? Does race matter more in the approval of black mayors or white mayors? These are some of the questions that will be addressed in this chapter.

We have already observed that race, racial context, and some racial attitudes affect certain performance evaluations and may therefore influence mayoral approval indirectly. Next we move to the second stage of the model in Figure 1.1 and estimate the direct effects of racial factors and performance measures on mayoral approval.

Performance Dimensions and Mayoral Approval—A Bivariate Look

Are citizens' evaluations of conditions in their cities related to approval of the mayor? The performance model is based on a steady increase in mayoral approval as opinions about performance improve. Our first look is a series of simple correlations between the eight performance dimensions and mayoral approval across the four cities (Table 6.1).

Table 6.1 Performance Dimensions and Mayoral Approval (Pearson Correlations)[a]

Performance Dimensions	*New Orleans*	*Detroit*	*Charlotte*	*Chicago*
Services	0.31***	0.45***	0.41***	0.48***
Police	0.23***	0.36***	0.35***	0.45***
General Evaluations	0.30***	0.36***	0.21***	0.38***
Economy	0.26***	0.30***	0.21***	0.39***
Schools	0.28***	0.23***	0.23***	0.28***
Transportation	0.21***	0.31***	0.20***	0.44***
Safety	0.10*	0.14**	0.11*	0.22***
Crime Decreasing	0.15**	0.18***	0.05	0.26***
Race (Black)	0.31***	-0.22***	-0.22***	-0.20***

* $p < 0.05$
** $p < 0.01$
*** $p < 0.001$

[a] These correlations are based on the pooled black and white samples from each city. They are not based on representative cross-sectional samples. The issue of different relationships between performance and approval among blacks vs. whites will be dealt with later in this chapter.

The most obvious conclusion is that virtually all of the citizen performance measures are significantly related to approval of the mayor in the predicted direction in all of the cities. That is, the more highly someone regards an aspect of performance, the more likely he or she is to approve of the mayor. This pattern is exactly consistent with the performance model.

The Services dimension has particularly high correlations with mayoral approval across all of the cities. This measure consists of ratings of specific city services such as control of abandoned housing, health services, litter and trash control, parks and recreation, pollution, and others, along with a general rating of the "overall level of government services." The Services dimension is unique in both its scope and diversity, which may explain its strong relationship to approval of the mayor.

To get a better idea of what these correlations mean, Figures 6.1a and 6.1b graphically present the differences in mayoral approval across four levels of opinions about city Services in New Orleans and in Detroit.[1] The graphs contain only the "strongly approve" category of the mayoral approval variable, although all of the categories of approval are used in computing the correlation coefficients. The purpose of these graphs is to demonstrate the different meaning of lower vs. higher correlation coefficients. The correlation between Services and mayoral approval is weakest in New Orleans (0.31) and strongest in Chicago (0.48). And, as is apparent in Figures 6.1a and 6.1b, the difference between the mayoral approval level of the lowest and highest quartiles of opinion on city services is greater in Chicago than in New Orleans.

The Police, Economy, and General Evaluations are also substantially related to mayoral approval, although not as consistently across the cities as Services. Originally, we predicted that the Police and the Economy would have relevance for mayoral approval because presidents and governors are judged on economic conditions, and because crime is often cited in public opinion surveys as the most urgent problem facing urban citizens. That prediction is borne out with the bivariate correlations; the correlations of Police evaluations with mayoral approval range from 0.23 to 0.45, and the Economy is correlated at 0.21 to 0.39 (Table 6.1). Again, graphs better demonstrate the relationships between these performance measures and approval of the mayor. In New Orleans where the relationship of attitudes toward the Police and mayoral approval is the weakest, the difference in strong mayoral approval between the lowest and highest quartiles of Police

[1] The Services measure has been collapsed from thirty-six categories into four categories to make graphing possible. The full thirty-six categories are used in computing the correlations and in the upcoming multivariate analysis.

evaluations is 20 percent. In contrast, in Chicago where the relationship of attitudes toward the Police and mayoral approval is the strongest, the difference between the lowest and highest quartiles of Police evaluation is 55 percent.

Regarding the Economy and General Evaluations, similar patterns can be observed in the graphs. The higher the correlation between the performance measure and mayoral approval, the greater the difference between those with lower opinions on the service compared to those with higher opinions on the service. The two performance dimensions with the lowest correlations, the Economy and General Evaluations in Charlotte, both 0.21, are characterized by no steady upward trend in mayoral approval across the quartiles of opinion on the performance measure.

Normally, mayors do not have responsibility for the public school system, which is typically run by an independent board and superintendent. However, as a result of low performance, particularly in economically disadvantaged areas, schools have been the focus of media attention, reform measures, and new state and national policies. In fact, how to improve public education is probably the most consistently high profile policy debate of the past thirty years. The debate is particularly relevant to urban areas where schools are often classified as poor performers. Urban newspapers regularly report on the latest trend in standardized test scores, the poor physical conditions in schools, and the violence that spills over from the streets into the classrooms. The media and political attention paid to urban public schools results in the public judging the quality of life in its community partly on the basis of its perceptions of the public schools. In two of our cities, Chicago and Detroit, the formerly elected school boards are now appointed by the mayor in a last ditch attempt to gain control of a corrupt or inept school administration (Wong and Shen 2003), thereby giving the mayor a key leadership role in school reform. However, in all of our cities, regardless of the formal structure, the bivariate relationships seemingly reveal that the chief urban executive takes some blame or credit for the quality of the schools.

Transportation is another performance dimension that has a predicted bivariate relationship to mayoral approval. Citizen evaluations of traffic control, the streets, and public transportation comprise the Transportation dimension. Getting around is a high priority for urban residents, whether in their own automobile or public transit, and problems with transportation are likely to be encountered on a daily, or at least weekly, basis. It should be no surprise that the relationship of Transportation evaluations to mayoral approval is highest in the largest city, Chicago, which arguably has the worst traffic problem among these four cities. Again we see the "up close and personal" nature of performance at the local level that makes it distinct from state or national performance.

Given the prominence of crime as a problem in urban areas, we originally thought that feelings of Safety and perceptions of whether Crime is increasing or decreasing would be more connected to mayoral approval. But these are the performance measures with the weakest relationships to approval of the mayor. We noted previously our reservations about the measure of Safety. The Safety scale is composed of questions that ask, "how safe do *you feel*?" as opposed to "how safe *is it*?" People have a natural protective tendency to believe that they, personally, are not in serious danger, but at the same time they believe that the city is not a safe place—there is danger "out there." The Safety questions are probably capturing both of these sentiments, but a judgment about the overall safety of the city, which we do not have, is more likely to be related to mayoral approval.

For different reasons, the Crime question may not be capturing performance in the area of crime as well as we had hoped because it asks whether respondents think crime has increased, decreased, or stayed the same over the past year. It is a question about a trend as opposed to a question about the current situation. Regardless of the measurement problem, the Crime question does have the predicted relationship to mayoral approval in three of the four cities.

Race and Mayoral Approval—The Bivariate Relationship

Racial polarization in mayoral approval exists in all four cities as we would expect given their racial histories. In a previous chapter we presented a table displaying the different levels of approval among whites vs. blacks in these cities (Table 4.2). But at that time we did not make an explicit comparison of the race/approval relationship to the performance/approval relationships. The correlations between being black (labeled Race) and mayoral approval are in the last row of Table 6.1 and indicate that race has a bivariate relationship with mayoral approval that is comparable to the bivariate relationships of approval with the individual performance measures. That is, race does not have clearly lower nor higher correlations with mayoral approval than the performance measures. Graphs of the racial polarization in mayoral approval emphasize the black/white differences in these cities (Figure 6.1i and 6.1j). There are large differences in the percent "strongly approving" of the mayor depending on the race of the respondent: 34 percent in New Orleans, 26 percent in Detroit, 30 percent in Charlotte, and 23 percent in Chicago.

a

City Services - New Orleans
(r = .31)
% Strongly Approve
100
80
60
40
20
0
27
32
45
57
1st Quartile
2nd Quartile
3rd Quartile
4th Quartile
Evaluations of City Services

b

City Services - Chicago
(r = .48)
% Strongly Approve
100
80
60
40
20
0
19
27
53
83
1st Quartile
2nd Quartile
3rd Quartile
4th Quartile
Evaluations of City Services

c

Police Evaluations - New Orleans
(r = .23)
% Strongly Approve
100
80
60
40
20
0
27
40
48
47
1st Quartile
2nd Quartile
3rd Quartile
4th Quartile
Evaluations of Police

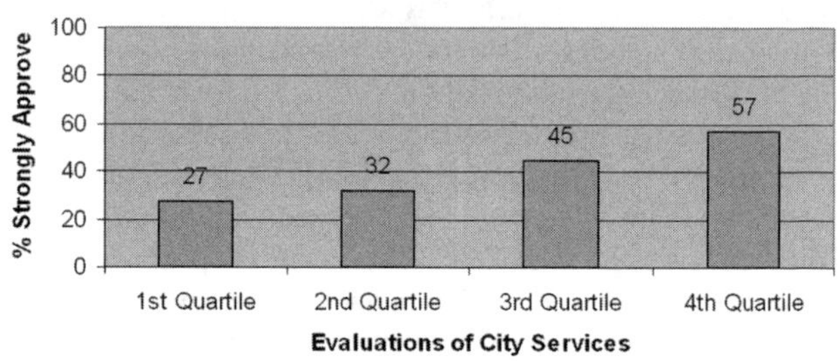

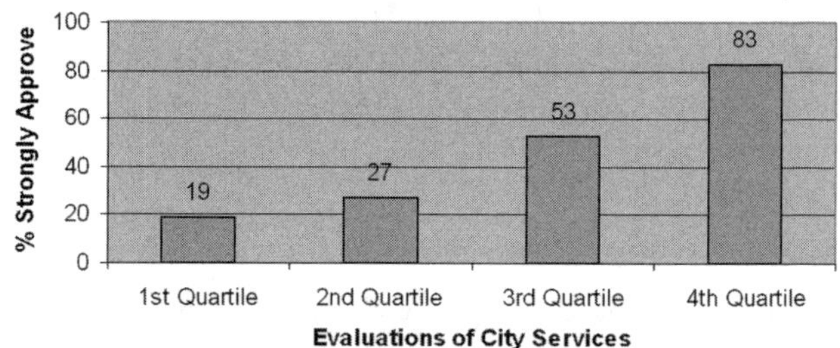

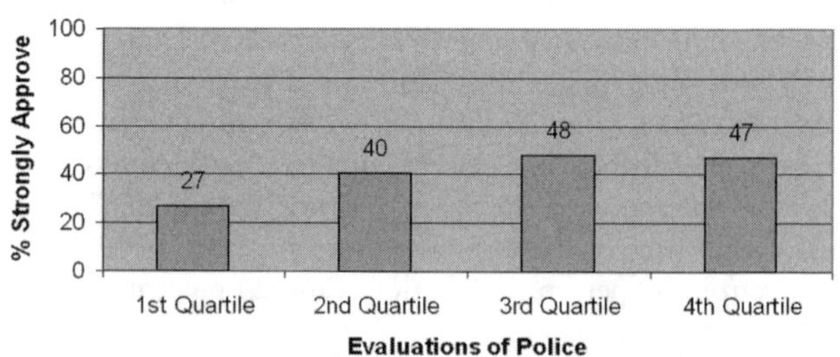

d

Police Evaluations - Chicago
(r = .45)
% Strongly Approve
100
80
60
40
20
0
20
44
53
75
1st Quartile
2nd Quartile
3rd Quartile
4th Quartile
Evaluations of Police

e

Economy - Charlotte
(r = .21)
% Strongly Approve
100
80
60
40
20
0
29
51
45
57
1st Quartile
2nd Quartile
3rd Quartile
4th Quartile
Evaluations of the Economy

f

Economy - Chicago
(r = .39)
% Strongly Approve
100
80
60
40
20
0
28
40
58
62
1st Quartile
2nd Quartile
3rd Quartile
4th Quartile
Evaluations of the Economy

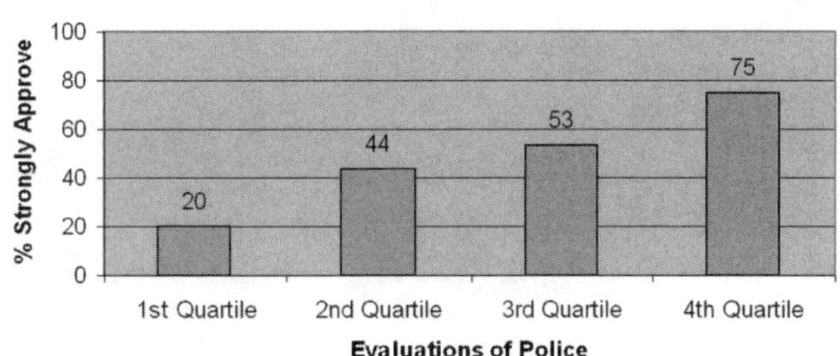

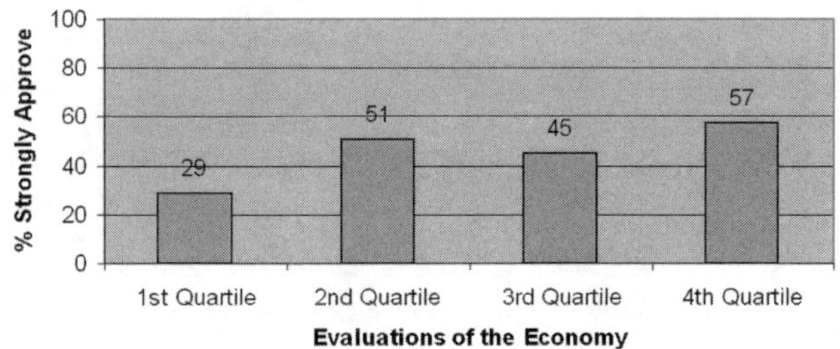

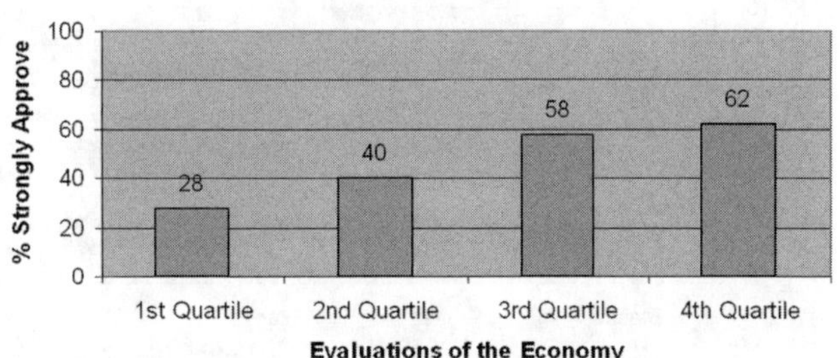

g

General Evaluations - Charlotte
(r = .21)
% Strongly Approve
100
80
60
40
20
0
29
48
47
52
1st Quartile
2nd Quartile
3rd Quartile
4th Quartile
General Evaluations

h

General Evaluations - Chicago
(r = .38)
% Strongly Approve
100
80
60
40
20
0
33
38
71
87
1st Quartile
2nd Quartile
3rd Quartile
4th Quartile
General Evaluations

i

Race
% Strongly Approve
100
80
60
40
20
0
71
37
38
64
Blacks
Whites
Blacks
Whites
New Orleans (r = .31)
Detroit (r = -.22)

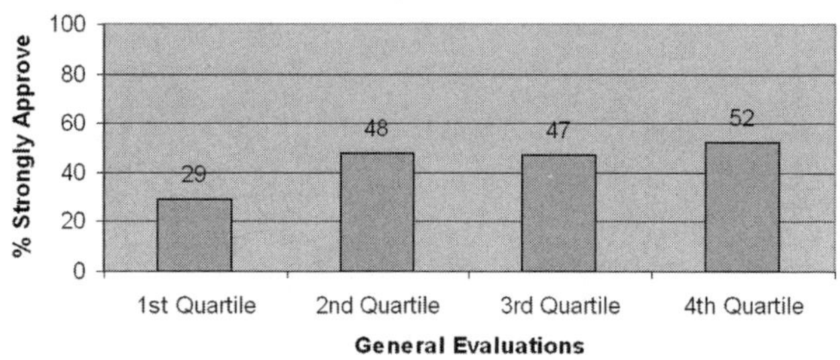

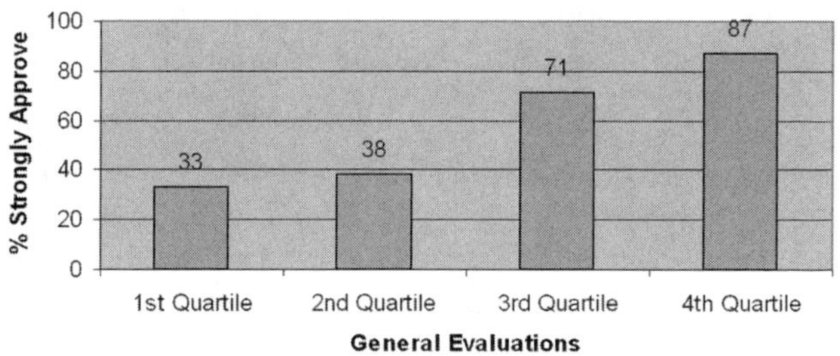

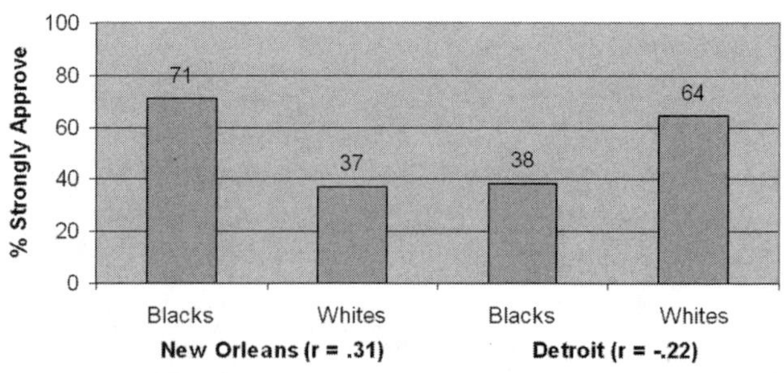

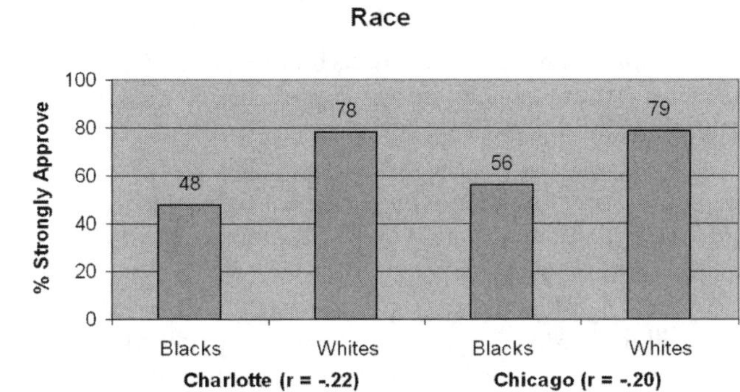

Figure 6.1 Selected Performance Measures, Race, and Mayoral Approval

One of our original hypotheses was that race would have a greater impact on the approval of black mayors than on the approval level of white mayors. The reasoning was simply that black mayors represent an exception to the norm of white executives and thus call attention to race. The bivariate correlations in Table 6.1 do not support this hypothesis; the correlations between respondent's race and approval are very similar in three of the cities, and only slightly higher in New Orleans. However, the upcoming multivariate analysis is a more accurate test of this hypothesis.

Based on the bivariate correlations, no performance measure has a stronger connection to mayoral approval in the majority white cities than in the majority black cities. Even though we might have expected that the crime-related performance measures would be more important in the majority black cities, such was not the case. The performance measures are related to mayoral approval in idiosyncratic ways that probably reflect events in that particular urban area.

Performance in the Multivariate Model

While the bivariate correlations of race and performance with mayoral approval provide an interesting initial look at what is related to approval, they cannot answer the question about the relative *independent* effects—the unique impact of race and the unique impact of performance. Nor do the bivariate correlations take into account the controls we have used previously, such as black neighborhood, income, education, gender, age, party identification, ideology and race of interviewer. We must use a multivariate technique to isolate the influences of race and performance on mayoral approval that are not contaminated by the relationships between race and performance observed in the last chapter or by relationships of race and performance with the controls.

The most appropriate multivariate technique in this case is some sort of ordered regression model, either ordered probit or ordered logit. These are the preferred techniques when the dependent variable consists of ordered categories. Since our dependent variable, mayoral approval, has four categories ranging from strongly disapprove to strongly approve, it fits the criterion for ordered regression nicely.[2] We realize that some readers may be "glazing over" at this point, but as we proceed we will translate ordered regression into plain English and into graphs in order to express results. We think the reader will find ordered regression a surprisingly user friendly method.

Performance does indeed influence mayoral approval above and beyond race. The ordered logit models of mayoral approval, including race and all of the performance dimensions, are presented in Table 6.2.

Table 6.2 Models of Mayoral Approval (ordered logit)

Y= Mayoral Approval	*New Orleans*	*Detroit*	*Charlotte*	*Chicago*
Race (Black)	1.21***	-0.77**	—	—
Services	3.66***	4.03***	3.43**	1.93*
Police	1.74**	1.50*	3.09**	1.86**
Schools	—	0.72[a]	1.22*	—
Economy	—	1.56**	—	2.17***
Safety	—	—	—	0.82[a]
Crime Decreasing	—	0.45[a]	—	—
Transportation	—	—	—	1.70*
Black Neighborhood	—	—	—	—
Threshold 1	1.03	1.68	2.37	1.22
Threshold 2	1.79	2.43	3.38	2.27
Threshold 3	3.57	4.47	5.95	4.35
N	398	416	369	410
Cragg & Uhler's R^2	0.34	0.34	0.31	0.37
BIC'	-51.26	-61.18	-25.12	-71.21

* $p < 0.05$
** $p < 0.01$
*** $p < 0.001$
[a] $p < 0.10$

Note: Dashes indicate insignificant ologit coefficients. Full models are in Table A.4.

[2] For those who want a more detailed description and the justification for not using linear regression, please refer to Long (1997).

First, the performance model receives support in all of the four cities because, depending on the city, two to five of the eight performance measures have significant independent effects on mayoral approval. Each of the significant performance measures impacts mayoral approval above and beyond all of the other performance measures, race, race of neighborhood, and the control variables. Second, all of the relationships between the performance measures and approval of the mayor are in the correct, positive direction, meaning that those who rate performance more highly are more likely to approve of the mayor. Thus, Hypothesis One, that performance is positively and strongly related to the approval of both white and black mayors is partially confirmed by these results. We say "partially" because the positive direction is confirmed, but we cannot easily determine the strength of the influence from ordered logit coefficients. Strength will be more apparent when we graphically illustrate the impact of each performance dimension.

The Special Meaning of "Strongly Approve"

Among the four responses to the mayoral approval, the answer, "strongly approve" is unique. Notice at the bottom of the columns for each city in Table 6.2 there are three thresholds with associated numbers. The numbers are important because they measure the distance between the four categories: strongly disapprove, disapprove, approve, and strongly approve. "Distance" in this context refers to the differences on all explanatory variables in the model between the respondents in that category vs. the next highest category. Threshold 1 is the distance between strongly disapprove and disapprove; threshold 2 minus threshold 1 is the distance between disapprove and approve; and threshold 3 minus threshold 2 is the distance between approve and strongly approve. Threshold 3 minus threshold 2 is the largest in all four cities, meaning that "strongly approve" is the most unique category of answer to the mayoral approval question.

In nonstatistical terms, strongly approve is different psychologically from the other answers. Responding "strongly approve" indicates an intensity of positive feeling that stands apart from the other answers. The basic "approve" response is probably psychologically cheap, an easy toss off answer that may not indicate much feeling one way or another. In Chapter 4 we noticed that the greatest differences between whites and blacks in all of these cities are in the "strongly approve" category (Table 4.2), indicating that it has more racial meaning than the other categories. As we examine the graphs in the following sections, the special status of "strongly approve" will be even more apparent.

City Services

The Services measure is particularly influential over mayoral approval, having the largest effect of all of the performance dimensions in all four cities. In the model, the Services dimension is the closest performance measure to an omnibus evaluation of conditions in the city. Most people are probably not focused on a single specific city service, but as a city's economy or budget grows, health services, housing, litter control, parks, recreation, and other aspects of life in the city improve, totaling to a general conclusion that the quality of life is getting better. And, of course, a downward spiral in city fortunes would have the opposite effect.

The influence of Services can best be understood graphically. Figure 6.2 plots the predicted probabilities of giving each of the four answers to the approval question depending upon how the respondent evaluates Services. Each line represents one of the four answers from strongly disapprove to strongly approve. For example, if someone in New Orleans gives all of the city Services the lowest possible rating (a score of 0), the probability of that person strongly approving (SA) of the mayor is about 0.12. But, if someone gives all of the city Services the highest rating, their probability of strongly approving of the mayor rises to 0.85—quite an increase. All of the lines can be similarly interpreted.

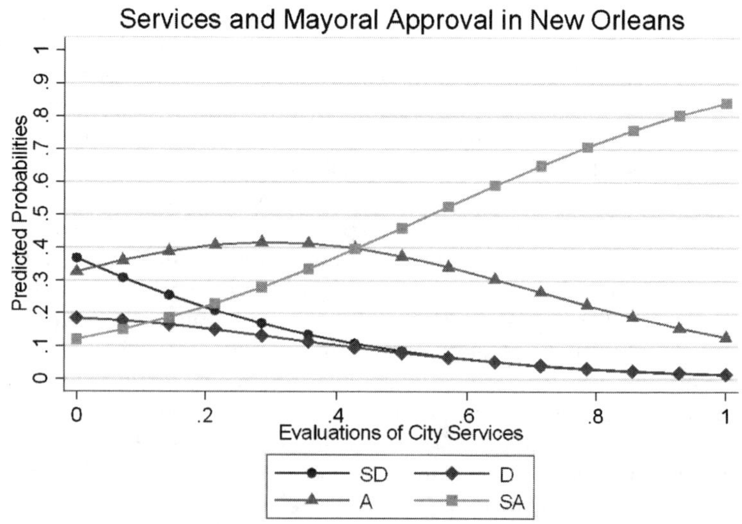

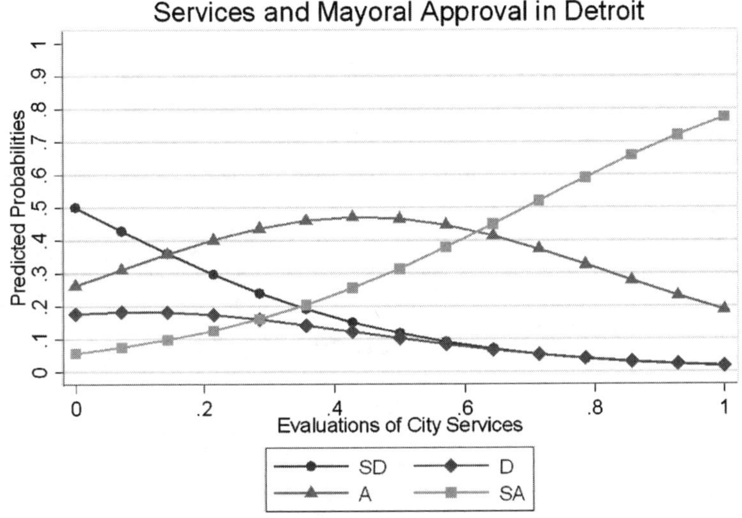
Services and Mayoral Approval in Detroit
Predicted Probabilities
0 .1 .2 .3 .4 .5 .6 .7 .8 .9 1
0 .2 .4 .6 .8 1
Evaluations of City Services
SD
D
A
SA

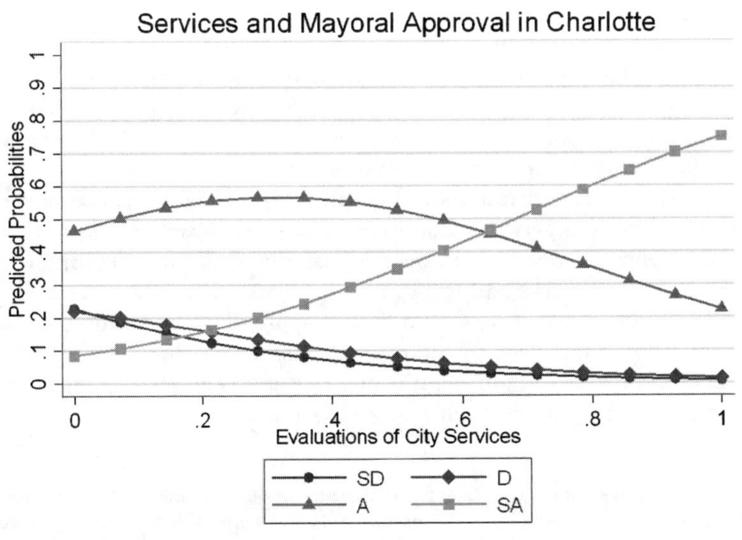
Services and Mayoral Approval in Charlotte
Predicted Probabilities
0 .1 .2 .3 .4 .5 .6 .7 .8 .9 1
0 .2 .4 .6 .8 1
Evaluations of City Services
SD
D
A
SA

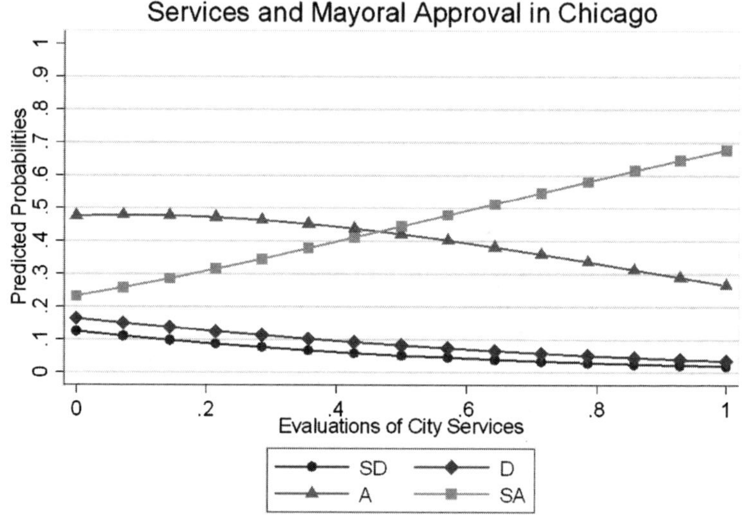

Figure 6.2 Impact of Evaluations of City Services on Mayoral Approval

Notice that, across all of the cities, the line representing "strongly approve" of the mayor has a unique pattern. It is much more affected by opinions on Services than any other response. In fact, only the "strongly approve" answer is positively affected by opinions on Services, suggesting that strongly approve is the only answer that really means *approve*.[3] Our suspicion that the basic "approve" answer is an easy, noncommittal response is confirmed, and thus, from this point forward the graphs focus on the "strongly approve" category as the true indicator of approval.

Moreover, recall that in the last chapter we observed a small racial effect on perceptions of Services. Consistent with past research, blacks were less positive about city Services in the two majority white cities. Thus, the differing views of blacks and whites toward Services are already factored in. When we observe that Services influence approval of the mayor, there is a small racial component to those evaluations in the two majority white cities. Another way of putting it is that race affects mayoral approval indirectly through opinions about municipal services.

[3] The positive coefficients in Table 6.2 associated with Services mean that as evaluations of Services become more positive, the mayor receives more approval in all cities. However, we can see from the graphs that this relationship is being produced by the strongly approve category.

The Police

Evaluations of the Police is the only dimension other than Services that influences approval of the mayor in all four cities. These opinions were expected to rank high as a predictor of mayoral approval; all of these cities have crime levels above the national average, and in all of these cities crime was mentioned most frequently as the "biggest problem" facing the city. Thus, it should come as no surprise that opinions about the Police feature largely in judging the mayor.

Evaluations of the police have a remarkably similar effect on the approval rating of three of the four mayors (Figure 6.3),[4] and all four mayors gain and lose popular support based on the attitudes of their citizens toward the Police. As was the case with city Services, opinions about the Police are racially polarized in the majority white cities. Specifically, blacks are less likely than whites to express favorable attitudes toward various aspects of policing. Thus, when Police evaluations influence approval of the mayor, race is already a part of that influence in the majority white cities. Race exerts an indirect effect on mayoral approval through opinions about the Police.

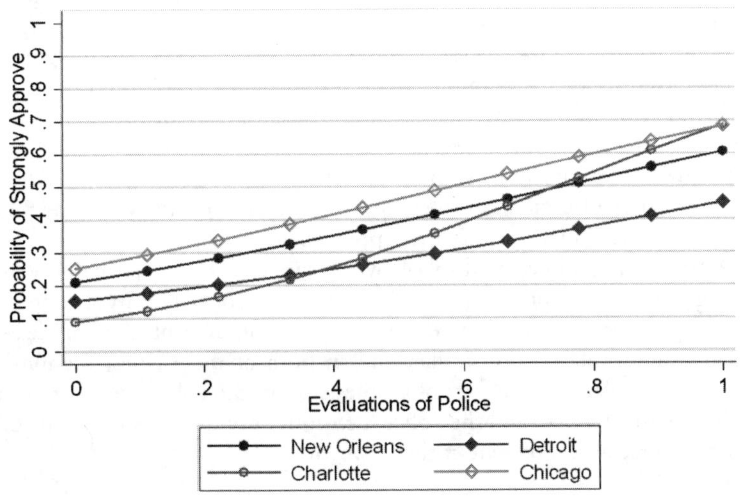

Figure 6.3 Impact of Evaluations of Police on Mayoral Approval

[4] The effects of Police evaluations are greater in Charlotte than in the other cities.

The Economy

Contrary to our expectations, the Economy did not impinge on mayoral approval across the board in all four cities. However, in the two cities where the Economy does influence approval, it ranks as one of the top three performance dimensions in terms of impact on the mayor. The economy is the aspect of performance most commonly utilized in national studies, and effects on presidential approval have been consistently found. The most likely explanation for why the local Economy is only sporadically influential is not that it is unimportant, but rather that there are other aspects of urban life, most notably crime and overall services, that compete with the Economy for public attention. Our use of seven measures of performance makes it more difficult for Economy to always emerge as the most prominent. With the possible exception of foreign affairs, the national economy typically has no performance competitors in the national studies. The question in most national studies is simply if and how much the economy affects presidential approval.

Another, more subtle, reason that the Economy is not is not influential across the board is that it is not likely to be felt by citizens everyday in the way that crime (as represented by the Police measure) and city Services are felt. The Economy, as represented by availability of jobs and likelihood of new businesses coming to the city, is more of a background condition, an important one, but at times less obtrusive than crime and city Services. Various factors can make a city's economy more or less salient to the public at any given time. For example, when the media or a political campaign highlight economic decline, such as closing businesses or job losses, or when publicity concerns a revitalized area of town or a new source of jobs, the economy is more likely to come to the forefront of people's minds. Any event or series of events that focus public attention on the economy will result in greater impact on mayoral approval.

Figure 6.4 graphically displays what happens to the probability of strongly approving of the mayor as opinions about the city Economy improve. In the two cities where the Economy is important, the impact on mayoral approval is quite similar, and in both of these cities, economic effects are similar to the effects of opinions about the Police. In contrast to evaluations of Services and the Police, perceptions of the city's Economy do not have a racial component in these two cities.

The Schools

Somewhat surprisingly, attitudes toward public Schools was the only other performance dimension affecting mayoral approval in more than one location. The impact of Schools is definitely smaller than Services, Police, or the

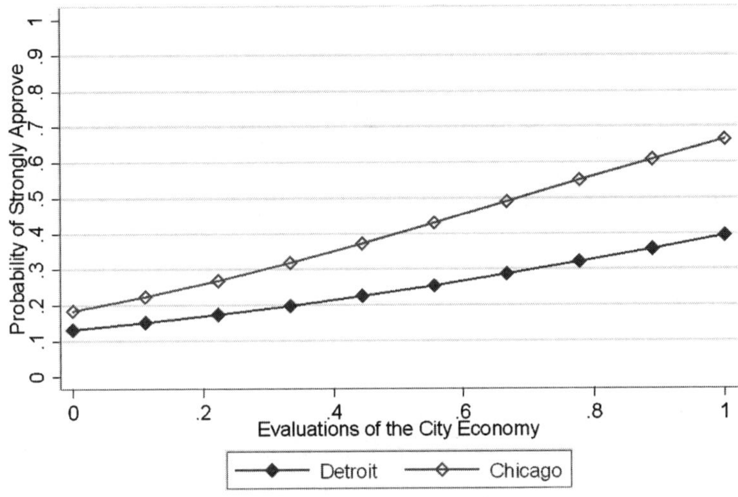

Figure 6.4 Perceptions of the City Economy and Mayoral Approval

Economy, and oddly, in Chicago, where the mayor has been given appointive power over the school board, evaluations of the Schools do not affect his approval. We suspect that Schools, like other aspects of performance, wax and wane in importance depending on the media attention and policy controversies surrounding them. At times the Schools are visible enough that the mayor reaps positive or negative consequences, and at other times they are not.

Figure 6.5 graphically displays how the probability of strongly approving of the mayor changes with opinions about the public Schools. You can readily see that the lines in the Schools graph are not as steep as the lines in the Economy, Police, or Services graphs, meaning that the mayors do not gain or lose as much from their constituents' evaluations of the Schools as they do from evaluations in the other areas.

Like opinions about Services and Police, evaluations of public Schools have a racial component in the background. In Chapter 5 we discussed our findings that in the two majority black cities, blacks are more positive than whites about the public Schools, which makes sense since blacks are more dependent on those schools. So when evaluations of the Schools affect the mayor in Detroit, race is already part of the picture.

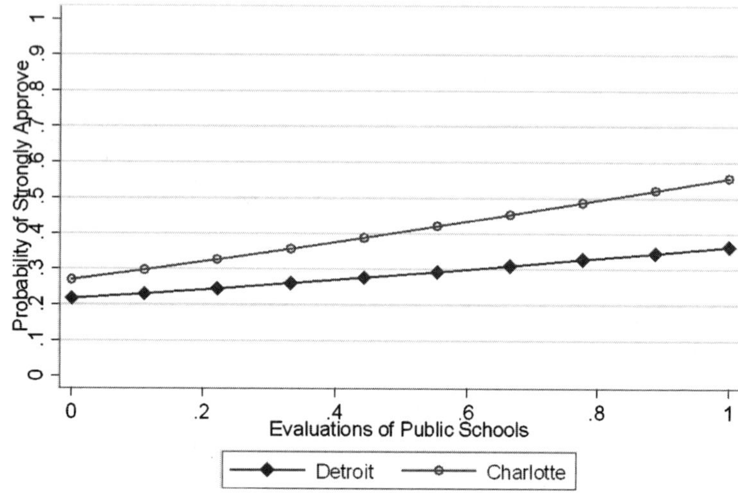

Figure 6.5 Impact of Evaluations of Public Schools on Mayoral Approval

Other Dimensions of Performance

Each of the remaining three dimensions of performance—Safety, the Crime trend, and Transportation—affect approval of the mayor in only one location, but they are still evidence of the performance model of mayoral approval. As mentioned above, it is likely that the impact of some aspects of performance varies over time and across locales depending on circumstances and events.

Why General Evaluations were Excluded

Readers may wonder at this point what happened to the General Evaluations performance measure. General Evaluations are excluded from the models of mayoral approval because they are likely to be affected by mayoral approval, creating a situation of mutual causation. People who approve of the mayor probably respond more positively when asked about the general direction of the city, and, in turn, people who have positive views of the general direction of the city give the mayor a higher rating. Reciprocal causation is undesirable because the estimates of influence will be inflated.

Because this is a cross-sectional study, we have no hard evidence of which opinion, General Evaluations or approval of the mayor, comes first. The General Evaluations questions are arguably more prone to these reciprocal effects than the more specific performance measures. Whether one likes or dislikes the mayor is much more likely to affect how respondents answer general questions than it is to affect specific questions about the streets, the crime trend, opportunities for employment, and most of the items comprising the performance dimensions. The specific items are simply less susceptible to psychological adjustments. So, taking a conservative approach, we excluded General Evaluations from the final models of mayoral approval.

Race in the Multivariate Model

In spite of seven performance measures and six demographic controls, race remains a highly significant determinant of mayoral approval in the two majority black cities, but not the two majority white cities (Table 6.2). That is, regardless of what someone thinks of Services, the Police, Schools, etc. and regardless of his or her neighborhood racial composition, economic status, party identification, ideology, age or other characteristics; in the two majority black cities race still affects how that person views the mayor. Such a result is quite impressive, but highly consistent with Hypothesis Two that

> race will have direct and independent effects on mayoral approval, regardless of evaluations of performance evaluations, and these effects are expected to be greater in the case of black mayors.

The greater influence of race on mayoral approval in the majority white cities is consistent with the theoretical basis of this research—that a majority black city with a black mayor increases the salience of race, especially for whites, thereby increasing its impact on approval of the mayor.

The best way to illustrate the unique impact of race in the majority black cities is to compute the predicted probabilities of approving and disapproving of the mayor for both blacks and whites. The probabilities in Table 6.3 can be interpreted as follows: For the "average" black person in New Orleans, the probability of strongly approving of the mayor is 0.54. By "average person" we mean a person with the average income, age, education, etc., and having average ratings on all of the performance measures. A white person with the all of the same average characteristics would have a 0.26 probability of strongly approving of the mayor, resulting in a black/white difference of 0.28. The same comparison can be made in Detroit resulting in a 0.15 difference between blacks and whites in the probability of strongly approving of the mayor. All of the characteristics except race are held constant so we can clearly see the independent impact of race alone. Both of these racial differences are quite significant when you consider that the comparisons are being made between people with identical characteristics on all of the other variables.

Table 6.3 Race and Predicted Mayoral Approval (based on the ordered logit model)

New Orleans	*Strongly Disapprove*	*Disapprove*	*Approve*	*Strongly Approve*
Blacks	0.06	0.06	0.33	0.54
Whites	0.19	0.14	0.41	0.26
Difference	*0.13*	*0.08*	*0.08*	*0.28*
Detroit	*Strongly Disapprove*	*Disapprove*	*Approve*	*Strongly Approve*
Blacks	0.19	0.14	0.46	0.21
Whites	0.10	0.09	0.45	0.36
Difference	*0.09*	*0.05*	*0.01*	*0.15*
Charlotte	*Strongly Disapprove*	*Disapprove*	*Approve*	*Strongly Approve*
Blacks	0.05	0.07	0.52	0.37
Whites	0.03	0.05	0.45	0.47
Difference	*0.02*	*0.02*	*0.07*	*0.10*
Chicago	*Strongly Disapprove*	*Disapprove*	*Approve*	*Strongly Approve*
Blacks	0.06	0.09	0.43	0.42
Whites	0.04	0.06	0.37	0.53
Difference	*0.02*	*0.03*	*0.06*	*0.11*

The largest differences between blacks and whites are in the strongly approve category. This response is the most valid measure of true approval because it requires the respondent to state approval with some degree of conviction. However, there are also notable racial differences in the strongly disapprove category. These two black mayors seem to elicit strong feelings, one way or another, based on race.

Detroit violates our expectations because white citizens are more likely to strongly disapprove of the black mayor than black citizens. Black constituents perceived Detroit's mayor, Dennis Archer, to be somewhat "white" in that he courted the white business community and focused on economic development. In the eyes of many black citizens, the focus on economic development was at the expense of black community interests. However, Dennis Archer's case is theoretically important. In spite of his policies, he was still black, therefore black citizens had expectations that he would represent their interests better than he did. Whites, also taking note of Archer's race, approved of him because of his policies and style, but not as intensely as they would have if he had been white. The point remains that black mayors, just by virtue of their race, create more racial polarization in their popularity than white mayors, and the racial polarization exists regardless of perceptions of performance.

A Summary Comparison of Performance and Race

Now that we know that both performance and race influence whether citizens approve of the mayor, we can compare their relative effects. Which is more important, race or performance? In the majority white cities the answer is easy; performance is clearly more influential because race is not even significant. However, in the majority black cities the comparison is not a simple one to make since there are seven measures of performance, some of which have little or no impact on approval of the mayor, and some of which have significant impact. One approach is to examine what happens to the overall quality of the model if we remove race, then examine what happens to the quality of the model if we remove performance.

The best overall indicators of the quality of a model are goodness of fit measures, in this case, Cragg and Uhler's R^2 and the Bayesian Information Criterion (BIC'). Cragg and Uhler's R^2 is analogous to R^2 in the linear regression model (Long and Freese 2003, 92), so readers familiar with regression will be comfortable with this coefficient. However, among those who use ordered regression models it is preferable to use some form of the BIC' (Rafferty 1996). What readers need to know is that larger R^2's are desirable, and larger and *negative* BIC's are desirable. By "desirable" we mean that the models are likely to represent what is actually happening in the observed data.

To illustrate, the model of mayoral approval in Chicago has the best overall fit; the R^2 is the highest, and the BIC' is the most negative. In contrast, the fit of the model in Charlotte is the lowest, as indicated by the lowest R^2 and the lowest negative BIC'.

In order to compare the influence of race vs. performance, we will begin with the full model goodness of fit measures and observe the effects of dropping race, then the effects of dropping performance. With seven performance measures and only one simple measure of race, it may seem that we are "stacking the deck" in favor of performance, and indeed, we do expect that performance will have a greater influence than race on approval of the mayor. However, the study of politics in racially diverse or majority black urban areas has been so focused on race that to show that mayors in these four settings are judged on performance is a new contribution. Also, the richness and complexity of "performance" at the local level incline us to expect that the performance measures will have more impact than race on mayoral approval.

Performance does a better job of predicting mayoral approval than race in all four cities (Table 6.4). The quality of the model is reduced considerably when we exclude the seven performance dimensions. Using the more familiar R^2 measure and beginning with the full model, the goodness of fit ranges from 0.31 to 0.37. However, when we exclude all of the performance measures, the goodness of fit drops to between 0.09 and 0.15. Similarly, the magnitude of the negative BIC's are reduced considerably without the performance measures, and three of the BIC's even become positive (indicating a very poor fit). Furthermore, the predictive power of all of the performance measures together is not clearly greater for the black mayors or the white mayors; all four mayors are judged heavily on performance.

Table 6.4 Comparing Race and Performance

	New Orleans	*Detroit*	*Charlotte*	*Chicago*
BIC′				
Full Model	-51.26	-61.18	-25.12	-71.21
Dropping Race	-35.91	-56.47	Insig.[a]	Insig.
Difference	*15.34*	*4.71*	*Insig.*	*Insig.*
Dropping Performance	-3.73	11.32	21.74	14.23
Difference	*47.53*	*72.50*	*46.86*	*56.98*
Cragg & Uhler's R^2				
Full Model	0.34	0.34	0.31	0.37
Dropping Race	0.29	0.32	Insig.	Insig.
Difference	*0.05*	*0.02*	*Insig.*	*Insig.*
Dropping Peformance	0.15	0.11	0.09	0.10
Difference	*0.19*	*0.23*	*0.22*	*0.27*

[a] The effect of dropping race was not computed in the white cities because it is insignificant and therefore assumed to be zero.

On the other hand, dropping race from the models either does not reduce their quality at all, or by much smaller amounts than occurs when dropping performance. When we exclude race, the goodness of fit does not decline at all in the majority white cities, which makes sense since race was insignificant in the model. In the majority black cities, the R^2 declines by small amounts—0.05 and 0.02. Results from the BIC's are similar. The difference between the full models and the models without race are much smaller than the differences when we drop performance.

In sum, performance matters more than race in evaluating both the black and white mayors. In spite of the racial influence on mayoral approval in the majority black cities, many citizens are observing other conditions in their city and giving the mayor credit or blame. Successful performance can and does overcome race as a predictor of approval. Combining strongly approve and approve, all four of these mayors had at least 62 percent approval from both races. Based on this evidence from four cities, we tentatively conclude that the performance model, which is commonly used to explain presidential and gubernatorial approval, can be generalized to mayors.

Are Certain Performance Measures More Important to Whites or Blacks?

Given the different life circumstances of blacks and whites, it may be the case that certain performance measures matter more to one racial group than the other. For example, considering the lower economic status of blacks in these cities, maybe economic opportunities, measured in the Economy scale, matter more to blacks than whites. Or, since blacks are far more likely to attend the public schools, evaluations of those schools would weigh more heavily in their assessment of the mayor. However, all twenty-eight possible racial differences were tested, and only two passed the test of statistical significance.[5] Apparently, blacks and whites react alike to their perceptions of these urban conditions when deciding their opinion of the mayor.

This finding indicates more commonality between blacks and whites than we normally expect. The performance dimensions with the most impact on mayoral approval, Services, the Police, and the Schools, are equally important for whites' and blacks' evaluation of their mayor. And where economic outlook affects mayoral approval, its impact is the same for blacks and whites. Thus, these mayors can expect credit or blame biracially depending on how well or poorly citizens evaluate the quality of urban life.

Racial Attitudes and Mayoral Approval

We also expect the racial attitudes of both blacks and whites to influence mayoral approval. Our original Hypothesis Four predicts that conservative white racial attitudes are positively related to approval of white mayors and

[5] To test for racial differences in the impact of performance measures, interaction terms were computed for each city separately. The interaction terms took the form of race X Police, race X Services, and so on. They were entered separately into the models, and the results were largely null as described in the text.

negatively related to approval of black mayors. Hypothesis Six predicts that black consciousness is positively related to approval of black mayors and negatively related to approval of white mayors.

In the last chapter we found scant evidence that white racial attitudes affected the performance dimensions. In fact, the only aspect of performance that was influenced by white racial attitudes was evaluations of the Police. Specifically, whites with a greater sense of competition with blacks gave the Police lower evaluations in the two majority black cities. Furthermore, black racial attitudes were even less effective in predicting any of the performance measures.

The question now is whether these racial attitudes have direct effects on approval of these mayors. To test Hypotheses Four and Six, we estimated the multivariate models of mayoral approval with whites and blacks within each city separated and their respective racial attitudes included. The clear conclusion is that these racial attitudes have very little impact on mayoral approval. Of the sixteen estimates of the influence of white racial attitudes (four in each of four cities), only three reached statistical significance; and of the sixteen estimates of black racial attitudes, only one reached significance.

Again we are faced with the question of why racial attitudes are so weak when compared to race itself in affecting how citizens view their mayors. And again we return to the powerful nature of racial identification. Simply being black or white is a more important distinction than any attitudinal differences among whites or blacks. Now that the dependent variable is approval of the mayor, we have introduced a specific person whose race is well known and whose politics are frequently discussed in racial terms. This appears to activate simple racial identification and minimize intraracial differences.

This does not mean that racial attitudes have no effect whatsoever on approval of the mayor. Whites with conservative racial views were more negative toward the Police in the majority black cities, and evaluations of the Police are one of the most important influences on approval of the mayor. So, in the majority black cities, there exists a two-step process by which white racial attitudes affect the mayor. First, white racial attitudes influence opinions about the Police, then opinions about the Police influence approval of the mayor.

Racial Context and Mayoral Approval

We have seen that racial context, whether a city is majority white or majority black, matters. First, nearly all evaluations of performance are lower and more negative in the majority black cities than the majority white cities, which should not be surprising given the objective quality of life differences in these cities. Second, race itself affects opinions about the city Services and the Police, but only in the majority white cities. Third, whites with the most antiblack racial attitudes are more negative toward the Police in the majority black cities but not in the majority white cities. And finally, race has more direct impact on mayoral approval in the majority black cities. In sum, racial context has proven to be a crucial background factor because blacks and whites react differently to these two environments.

Does racial context directly affect mayoral approval? It would certainly be simple if we could say that approval ratings for the mayors in the majority white cities are higher because the objective conditions are better, but such is not the case. The actual situation is more complex. Table 6.3 presents the predicted probabilities of approving or disapproving the mayors by race and by city. Remember that these probabilities already control for all of the performance measures, socioeconomic status, and other demographic factors, so they are the unique effects of the racial environment.

Within-race divisions characterize the majority black cities more than the majority white cities. First consider Detroit, the majority black city where whites approve of the black mayor more than blacks. In this minority context the black citizens are very divided within themselves on opinion of the mayor; 20 percent are predicted to strongly disapprove and 20 percent are predicted to strongly approve. In fact, in Detroit, black approval is lower, and disapproval is higher, than in any of the four cities. A black mayor like Dennis Archer, with perceived "white" policies, divided the black electorate.

Within-race division also characterizes the other majority black city, New Orleans. But there the split is among whites. Like the blacks in Detroit, whites in New Orleans have the lowest probability of approving and the highest probability of disapproving than in any of the four cities. Marc Morial was a black mayor who was closely identified with the black community and black interests. His image produced a predictably negative reaction from the antiblack segment of the white electorate.

In contrast, more within-race consensus about the mayor characterizes the majority white cities. The strongly approve probabilities are more similar within both blacks and whites, and neither racial group is very likely to disapprove of either of these mayors.

What is it about the majority black cities that divides one of the racial groups within itself more than in the majority white cities? First, we should note that any explanation is very tentative, given the limitations of a study of only four cities. However, we believe that the explanation lies in the different objective conditions in white vs. black cities, in combination with the context of a black majority. According to the performance model, the objective conditions alone in many majority black cities would predispose some citizens to disapprove of the mayor, regardless of their race. In addition, a black mayor and black majority in the city call attention to race. Blacks have high expectations of a minority mayor, and therefore are either pleased or disillusioned depending how they perceive their interests are represented. Whites add their anxiety about being in the minority to the deteriorating quality of life in the city and lay blame on a black mayor who they believe is too attentive to the minority community. So the poor objective conditions pull whichever racial group feels most disadvantaged by the current black administration into disapproving of the mayor, e.g., blacks in Detroit and whites in New Orleans.

On the other hand, a better quality of life characterizes the majority white cities, and in these cities both racial groups are in their normal positions. In these circumstances blacks will typically think less of the white mayor than whites, but they are not facing a perceived "betrayal" from a member of their own race.

Summary

This chapter has presented a comprehensive test of the performance model of mayoral approval, complete with seven measures of performance, the complications posed by race, and standard demographic controls. What emerges is a complex picture of how perceptions of conditions in the city and racial factors combine and sometimes interact to produce mayoral popularity. Most importantly, the performance model receives resounding support; the predictive power of the seven performance measures combined is quite impressive, and, as expected, higher evaluations of performance translate into greater mayoral approval. In short, the performance model can be generalized to the local level.

Some aspects of performance are clearly more important than other aspects when evaluating the mayors. An omnibus measure of city Services has the greatest impact on approval of the mayor in all four cities. Eight specific services and one general measure comprise this scale, so it makes sense that such a wide ranging measure would have important consequences for the mayor's popularity. The only other performance dimension affecting mayoral approval across the board is evaluation of the Police, which was expected to be influential given the salience of crime in these urban areas. Less important, but still significant in two of the cities, are perceptions of the quality of the public Schools and the Economy.

Given the prominence of the economy in national studies of executive approval, we originally expected the local Economy to play the same role in all four cities. However, it seems that the local Economy is obtrusive or unobtrusive depending on events and circumstances, although it is almost certainly a constant background factor.

Overall, performance is a far better predictor of mayoral approval than race in all four cities—a positive finding both theoretically and normatively. Theoretically, it constitutes strong confirmation of the performance model. Normatively it indicates that, while race has a role, it is not the dominant role. There are other positive normative findings as well. Black and white citizens react alike to perceptions of performance in their city, racial attitudes have little direct effect on mayoral approval, and no performance dimension was more important in evaluating black mayors or white mayors. All of these indicate commonalities in how black and white residents of these cities evaluate their mayors.

The racial environment has been an important background and conditioning factor throughout this study. First, as mentioned above, a black environment gives race more influence over mayoral approval. Second, the black environments seem to divide one of the racial groups within itself more than the white environments, a pattern we tentatively attribute to the less desirable objective conditions in minority cities and the extra attention drawn to race, which alienates a segment of one of the racial groups.

In sum, while the performance model of mayoral approval in these racially diverse cities is confirmed, it is not simple. Race, racial attitudes, and racial context complicate the model via either direct effects on mayoral approval, conditioning effects, or indirect effects through evaluations of performance.

Chapter 7
Conclusion and Discussion

The notion that citizens both blame and give credit to executives for what they perceive to be conditions in the nation, state, or locale is the basis of the performance model of executive approval. This model has been demonstrated amply at both the national and state levels, where evaluations of economic performance and other aspects of performance influence approval of governors and presidents. However, it was unconfirmed as to whether the model could be applied to local executives as well. The study of performance and approval at the local level is important because local government has more impact on people's everyday lives; local conditions are immediate and personal compared to conditions in the more abstract state or nation.

However, the presence of black executives complicates the performance model at the local level, which inevitably introduces race and racial factors. Race, meaning the black/white distinction, is the most prominent social, cultural, and economic division in this country, the "divide without peer" (Kinder and Sanders 1996, 27). Race and racial considerations have the power to alter the way citizens view themselves, their communities, and their leaders, so any model of mayoral approval must include race and racial factors.

The term, "race," has a broad theoretical meaning in this research. In addition to the traditional demographic and its accompanying racial identification, race also means racial attitudes and racial context. Among whites, racial attitudes are some form of antiblack racism, and among blacks the relevant racial attitude is some form of black consciousness. Racial context is the racial composition of the environment, whether it is majority white or majority black. The racial context in which blacks and whites live affects their attitudes and behaviors. So, whether the city's population is predominantly black or white must be part of the performance model of mayoral approval.

The theoretical basis for many of the hypotheses is social dominance theory and its corollary in the group conflict model of race relations. Social dominance theory posits that societies are organized around dominant and subordinate groups. The dominant group seeks to frame issues and to promote values to maintain its position, while the subordinate group attempts to attain a greater share of the status and privileges of the dominant group. Typically in America whites represent the dominant group, and blacks are socially, economically and politically subordinate. However, in areas of black empowerment, such as majority black cities with black mayors, the positions of the two racial groups are reversed, at least politically, a switch that has tremendous significance for both blacks and whites. Furthermore, according to the group competition model, blacks and whites perceive, to some degree, that gains by one group are losses for the other. Within the confines of a single city, the sense of competition is exacerbated because it is easy to see your race in competition with the other race for jobs, public offices, schools and neighborhoods. In sum, the sense of group competition, in combination with the perception of being dominant or subordinate, was expected to influence how both blacks and whites view the mayor and the quality of life in their city.

We proposed a model that interweaves race into the performance model of mayoral approval. First and foremost, and consistent with the national and state level studies, we expected performance to be a powerful predictor of mayoral popularity. Racial factors enter the model in several ways. We expected race and racial attitudes to influence perceptions of conditions in the city, and we expected those perceptions, which are the measures of performance, to impact mayoral approval. In addition to the indirect effects just described, we hypothesized that race and racial attitudes would influence approval of the mayor directly. We expected the third racial factor, racial context, to alter the nature of the relationships described above, and therefore serve as a conditioning factor.

We tested the model in two majority black cities with black mayors and two majority white cities with white mayors, cities chosen precisely because of their differences. In addition to the racial differences, two cities are southern and two are northern, one is a megacity, and one has a Republican mayor. The more different the cities are on race and other variables, the more confident we can be in the results because the conclusions have "survived" various types of settings. To protect against the possibility that the results are driven by one city, we imposed a rule that we would not offer up any finding unless it were true in either three of the four cities, the two majority white cities only, or the two majority black cities only. But, even with these adjustments, it is questionable whether it is possible to generalize the results. This question is left to future research.

Performance and Approval of the Mayor

The most important conclusion from the research is that perceptions of performance are a strong predictor of mayoral approval in all four cities, confirming that the basic performance model of executive approval applies at the local level. Moreover, the impact of performance evaluations on approval of the mayor in these four cities far exceeds the impact of race or racial attitudes. Normatively, this is a positive result because it means that improvements in conditions in the city will benefit the mayor regardless of his or her race, and regardless of the race of the constituents. Even more important, both blacks and whites give similar weight to performance when judging the mayor, and no particular type of performance was more important in judging black or white mayors. Thus, based on these four cities, there are more commonalities than differences in how blacks and whites decide their evaluations of the mayor.

It could be argued that the research is biased in favor of performance with the use of seven types of performance representing twenty-five individual indicators. No wonder race was less influential. The numerous measures of performance undoubtedly increased its overall power and made it difficult for race, or any other variable, to exert a similar impact. However, this is what constitutes performance at the local level. It is a more complex concept because of the variety of city conditions on which citizens can evaluate performance. The city's economy, crime, the police, safety, transportation, services and schools are all aspects of the quality of city life, and urban residents can personally observe these phenomena, as well as hear about them from friends, relatives, and the media. In addition to the rich content of performance, the personal nature of how citizens experience performance gives it extra power over evaluations of the mayor.

At the local level it is valuable to measure performance in a more detailed fashion than at the state or national level. There are similarities and differences across the four cities as to what specific aspects of performance affect the mayor. An omnibus measure of a variety of city Services has the greatest impact on mayoral approval in all cities, probably because it reflects an overall perception of city conditions. A second aspect of performance that is influential in all four cities is evaluations of the Police, which is predictable given the concern about crime in these urban areas. Beyond these two performance areas, the similarity across cities breaks down.

Perceptions of the city Economy, which was expected to be one of the most powerful predictors of mayoral approval across the board, was highly influential in two cities and inconsequential in the other two. This finding may seem contradictory to state and national studies in which the economy is influential in executive approval. The difference between the inconsistent local effects here and the steady effects nationally and statewide may be due to both the nature of economic performance at the local level and the methodology of the national and state studies. As described above, the local Economy is only one facet of the quality of life, and although it is very important, it competes with other conditions for public attention. The visibility of a city's economy to its citizens probably varies with events, sometimes becoming obtrusive, and at other times receding into the background. While omnipresent, the economy is not as noticeable on an everyday basis as city services or crime. In contrast, at the national level, the economy is front and center in the national media, rarely fading into the background. Moreover, research on presidential and gubernatorial approval does not pit economic evaluations against five or six other aspects of domestic performance, partly because people's opinions about the police, schools, crime, housing, parks, etc., only make sense at the local level.

It would be unrealistic to expect all of the aspects of quality of life to affect mayoral approval in all four cities. Events and circumstances will elevate or diminish the importance of single dimensions as illustrated by the unusual impact of Transportation in Chicago. In the megacity of Chicago, Transportation has an effect on mayoral approval that is very similar to the effect of the Economy. This seems strange until we consider the characteristics of transportation in Chicago. First, Chicago is by far the largest of our four cities; with a population of 2.9 million within the city limits, it is at least five times larger than Detroit, Charlotte, or New Orleans. With such a large population, the ability to get around to work and other activities is likely to be more difficult, and indeed Chicago, along with other large cities, is known for its traffic problems. Second, Chicago is the only city among our four with a commuter train system; the other cities rely on buses for public transportation. Commuter trains increase reliance on public transportation, and therefore it becomes a part of more people's lives. So the combination of traffic problems and a comprehensive commuter train system makes the Transportation dimension important in Chicago.

In sum, conditions in the city, what we have labeled "performance," is a crucial determinant of mayoral approval, but it is not the whole story in these racially divided cities. Race, the racial context, and to a lesser extent, racial attitudes play a role in citizens' evaluations of their mayor.

Race, Racial Context and Approval of the Mayor

Race influences mayoral approval independent of the performance measures, but only in the majority black cities, not in the majority white cities. Race affects approval regardless of a citizen's opinions of conditions in the city, the racial composition of his or her neighborhood, or his or her income, education, age, gender, or party identification. This was no surprise given the racial histories in these two majority black cities.

However, it was somewhat of a surprise to find absolutely no significant effects of race in the two majority white cities, both of which also have histories of racial conflict. Our tentative explanation is that extra attention is focused on race in a majority black context with a black leader because such a situation is a reversal of the normal racial power arrangement. The increased salience of race occurs among both blacks and whites. For blacks who are used to minority status and its accompanying economic, political, and social disadvantages, the election of one of their own to the office of mayor is a source of tremendous pride, particularly if the black mayor defeated a white candidate. Blacks expect that opportunities for members of their race will improve, and they will have greater access to jobs, public offices, city contracts, and other perks of political power. But most importantly, they believe that a majority black city administration will be much more responsive to their needs than a white administration.

In contrast, for whites, the transition represents something else altogether. Both of these majority black cities were once majority white, and although both have had black administrations for more than twenty years, whites still feel a loss of status when they find themselves in the minority. When whites are in the majority they are far less conscious of race than blacks; they lack a sense of racial identity because their culture and race *are* the social order. Sociologists have said that whites often feel a "sense of culturelessness and racelessness" (Doane 2003), a phenomena that has been labeled the "invisibility" of whiteness. Following this logic, when whites find themselves in the minority their racial identity quickly becomes "visible" to them and therefore more salient.

But race not only affects evaluations of the mayor; race also influences perceptions about conditions in the city. The performance model would be incomplete if it did not acknowledge that people view the city itself through a racial lens.

Race, Racial Context, and Performance Evaluations

Both blacks and whites observe conditions in their cities every day. Given the racial divide between blacks and whites on a myriad of issues and perceptions, it would be surprising if race did not color perceptions of city conditions to some extent. Our original expectation was that, due to their relative positions in society and possible differences in actual service delivery, whites would be more positive than blacks about evaluations of performance, and, we found that whites are more positive than blacks on two performance dimensions, city Services and the Police. The history of black abuse by police is long, and continued differential treatment of whites and blacks by police fuels the distrust of law enforcement among blacks.

Racial differences in perception of municipal Services are less easy to explain. We cannot use simple socioeconomic explanations because we have controlled for income and education. Also, living in a black (and presumably poor) neighborhood is also a control, so differences in neighborhood conditions are probably not the explanation. A third possibility is that black citizens, regardless of their economic status and their neighborhoods, are more aware of, and therefore more critical of, city services due to their family and friends who are users of those services. Another possibility is simply a negative global assessment of the city from the vantage point of a disadvantaged minority group.

Our original expectation stipulated that not only would blacks be more negative about city conditions than whites, but that the black/white difference would be accentuated in the majority white cities. In fact, the data showed that the greater black negativity regarding city Services and the Police was only present in the majority white cities and completely absent in the majority black cities. For an explanation we must return to the objective conditions that plague many majority black cities. Black residents are more negative about the quality of life in the majority black cities than in the majority white cities on six of the eight dimensions. These findings are an individual level version of the "hollow prize" thesis of Friesema (1969), that black mayors in majority black cities face economic conditions that make it nearly impossible to succeed, hence the phrase "hollow prize." For individual blacks, the majority black city is also something of a hollow prize as evidenced by their answers to questions about conditions in their city.

But, blacks' evaluations of the Services and the Police do not decline as much as whites' evaluations in the move from the majority white cities to the majority black cities. To find out why they do not decline as much, we return to the relative power positions of blacks and whites in American society. Blacks have long been excluded from the circles of power. Therefore, becoming the majority in the city and gaining ascendancy to the mayor's office mean that blacks can believe that access to government—and the accompanying jobs, patronage, and status—is available to them. Although reality has fallen short of expectations, blacks also believe that a black mayor and administration will ultimately improve their quality of life. These are the positive forces operating on blacks in the majority black cities that serve as a countervailing force to the depressed objective conditions in these cities. The net result is a smaller effect of racial context on evaluations of city Services and the Police among blacks.

In contrast, whites are losing on all fronts. They experience both the loss of real political power and a symbolic loss of status, even though they retain their economic privileges. On top of that, they observe the same deterioration of city conditions that blacks observe, which, when combined with the anxiety of a group accustomed to more status and privilege, produces a larger negative response.

The Changeable Effects of Performance Dimensions

Exactly what aspects of performance influence an executive's approval is a variable thing. At the presidential level, popularity is sometimes driven by domestic affairs, sometimes by foreign events, and at other times by scandal. The most salient events and conditions of the times similarly affect the popularity of mayors. Evaluations of Schools, the city Economy, the Crime trend, and Transportation all influence the approval of the mayor in only one or two of the cities. If there were more cities in the study, undoubtedly there would be an even greater variety of combinations of performance dimensions affecting the mayor.

Racial Attitudes and Performance Evaluations

We expected racial attitudes to influence perceptions about conditions in the city because there is within-race variation in how people view racial matters. With one exception racial attitudes proved to be largely irrelevant to evaluations of conditions in the city. The two measures of black racial consciousness, both used in previous research, are virtually unrelated to performance evaluations. Among whites, racial attitudes, as hypothesized, have more influence in the majority black cities than the majority white cities, but the effects on specific dimensions are sporadic and unpatterned, limiting our ability to draw conclusions.

Police evaluations are a glaring exception to the general conclusion of limited effects of racial attitudes. Police evaluations are influenced substantially by whites' sense of group competition with blacks, but only in the majority black cities. The magnitude of the influence is notable because it is greater than the impact of race itself on any of the performance measures. The tie between these white racial attitudes and opinions about the police is an interesting finding because it draws together the historic racialization of attitudes toward the police, the negative reaction of whites-as-minority, and the activation of white racial identity. Moreover, it makes sense that Police evaluations are most affected by whites' racial attitudes because Police are the institution that whites usually embrace as the protector of the social order. In a majority black context, especially one with a high murder rate, those whites with the greatest sense of racial group competition can be expected to turn against a majority black police force because they feel a loss of their social order and safety.

The Special Meaning of "Strongly Approve"

It is common to measure executive approval with an item that has four or five categories ranging from strongly disapprove to strongly approve, and occasionally the answers are only two categories, approve or disapprove. The assumption is that anyone who says "approve" is giving the executive a positive evaluation. Our findings indicate that this may not always be the case. The use of an ordered regression model made this discovery possible because, in simple terms, it produces probabilities for each of the four answers separately, in contrast to ordinary least squares (OLS), which produces a predicted score on the entire scale.

To our surprise, the answer "approve" was actually negatively related to performance evaluations. This can occur when an "approve" answer is a noncommittal toss off answer which, although it may contain some genuine approval, can also mean indifference, lack of any opinion, or a reluctance to say something negative. In most of these cases "approve" does not indicate true approval of the mayor. In contrast, "strongly approve" has the expected positive relationship to the performance measures, suggesting that it is the response that truly means approve. Further evidence of the validity of a "strongly approve" response lies in the racial polarization pattern in Table 4.4. The gap between blacks and whites is much greater in the "strongly approve" category than in the "approve" category. In fact, in three cities, there was no racial polarization in "approve" responses. Since we know from the histories of these mayors, from their elections, and from the racial differences in the "strongly disapprove" category that there is indeed a racial gap in approval, we can only conclude that approval with any conviction is only measured by a response of "strongly approve."

Researchers should probably take a closer look at measures of approval of any public official. Any measure that only gives citizens two choices, approve or disapprove, may be inviting measurement error because the approve answer is so contaminated with attitudes that fall short of a true positive evaluation of the official. Of course there are also those who do genuinely approve in the mix, but the evidence indicates that these are a minority of the approve category. At the very least, researchers should include some measure of intensity of approval. Beyond that, they should test their measures using some type of ordered regression model to estimate where on the scale genuine approval begins.

Approval vs. the Vote

Approving of an incumbent executive does not automatically translate into a vote for that incumbent. These two are positively related, but decidedly different concepts with distinct functions. Voting is a behavior that takes place in the emotionally heated atmosphere of a campaign. People pay more attention to the incumbent during the campaign and compare him or her to the challenger. In addition, the media are deluging the public with information and analyses of the performance and characteristics of both the incumbent and the challenger. The fundamental purpose of voting is to choose between competing candidates for a public office.

In contrast, approval is a running tally of how the electorate evaluates the incumbent. Approval can be measured in times of relative apathy or during a crisis; it can be measured frequently or only sporadically. Unlike elections, there is often no regularity to the appearance of approval readings. The media and other political actors use the results to take the political temperature of the incumbent. Some questions asked are: "Are the voters pleased or displeased?"; "Is the incumbent's approval increasing, decreasing or remaining stable?" and "Among what groups is he or she strong and among what groups is he or she weak?" While they might deny it, most incumbents pay close attention to their approval ratings because they represent political capital, or lack thereof, that can be used in promoting their agenda or their reelection.

In the best tradition of democracy, approval ratings are a way that, between elections, the public can influence the actions of an incumbent, and therefore influence public policy. Of particular importance is the trend in approval and how the incumbent interprets that trend. Approval that is increasing, or stable high approval, can be interpreted to mean that the electorate is, by and large, pleased with the way things are going—no major changes are called for. On the other hand, declining approval or persistent low approval, indicates the presence of a problem or problems that the incumbent should aggressively address. In this manner, approval ratings can enhance the operation of a democratic system in the periods between elections.

Limitations of the Research

The most serious limitation of this research is its basis in only four cities; it is fundamentally a four case study. There is no scientific or statistical basis for claiming generalizability to other racially diverse cities. Another approach would have been to use all cities above a certain population that have black mayors and a similar number of cities that have white mayors, and conduct equal numbers of black and white interviews in each group. Such an approach would enhance generalizability, and the sample would include the interesting case of black mayors in majority white cities. But the vast majority of these black mayors would be first time black mayors, and very few respondents would be from cities with second or third generation black leadership. We felt that having half of the sample coming from cities with long-term black leadership was more important because it more firmly addresses the question of how black mayors are judged when they are no longer a novelty.

Another problem with a broader sample of cities is that, unless the study is conducted over several years, many of the mayors would not have been in office long enough to be rewarded or punished for performance. For any executive there is a honeymoon period after their election or reelection when approval levels are artificially high. The electorate is giving the new mayor the benefit of the doubt, but only temporarily. This is not the appropriate time to conduct a study of how performance affects approval.

A second serious limitation of this research is the inability to measure the personal traits of these mayors. Performance is not the only reason people like or dislike the mayor. Mayors can be perceived as charismatic, trustworthy, warm and caring, or strong leaders; or they can be perceived as the opposite. Perceptions about these traits can and do exist independently of perceptions of performance like the phrases: "he's a crook, but he gets things done" or "I give her credit for (whatever), but I just don't like her." There are volumes of research demonstrating that candidate traits influence voting behavior (cf. Funk 1999; Miller and Shanks 1996; Niemi and Weisberg 2001). So, measures of these traits should be included in models of mayoral approval. Race certainly influences how people perceive the mayor's personal characteristics, but the relationship between personal traits and opinions about performance is not as clear. Most likely there are reciprocal effects between these two sets of attitudes; that is, opinions about personal traits influence perceptions of performance and vice versa. The implication for this research is that the performance indicators tap attitudes about personal traits, and there remains an unmeasured impact of personal traits on mayoral approval. Thus, the overall explanatory power of the model is less than it would have been if personal traits had been included.

Concluding Comments

It is normatively pleasing that citizen perceptions of performance affect these two black mayors and two white mayors alike. From the standpoint of democratic theory, mayors should be judged on the extent to which citizens are satisfied with conditions in their cities. In fact, it could be argued that the essence of democracy in our decentralized political system is the relationship of citizens to their local governments. However, in racially diverse settings, we must expect race to complicate matters and it does. Furthermore, the complications are not simple because they differ depending upon who holds political power.

All research raises more questions than it answers, and this is no exception. The most obvious next step is to extend the study of mayoral approval to other locations. These other locations should not be chosen on an ad hoc basis, but rather with an eye to creating variation on systemic variables, such as city size, city wealth, the political party in power, and racial composition. The role of performance and race in mayoral approval could be extended to cities with Latino mayors to determine if Latino ethnicity affects evaluations of performance and mayoral approval in the same fashion as being African American. Also, perceptions of the personal traits of the mayors need to be added to the model. Questions like: "How powerful are these compared to performance in predicting approval of the mayor?" and "How does race affect perceptions of personal traits?" need to be asked. The role of performance evaluations in mayoral elections is another natural extension of this research. Here questions like, "What is the web of relationships between performance evaluations, race or ethnicity, and vote?" are essential. All in all, the study of public opinion and local government using a variety of locations is a rich and largely untapped source of information on how citizens relate to government close to home.

Appendix

The Surveys

The Mayoral Approval Surveys were conducted between May and August 2000 in four cities—New Orleans, Detroit, Charlotte, and Chicago, by the University of New Orleans Survey Research Center. This project was funded by the National Science Foundation (Award #9986165). All of the surveys included registered voters only. Our research team interviewed nearly equal numbers of blacks and whites in each city in order to maximize variance on race. Thus, the samples from each city do not represent cross sections of each city's registered voters, but they do attempt to represent a cross section of whites or blacks in each city. In order to obtain the desired number of respondents from the minority race (whether white or black), first the cross section sample was exhausted. Then, areas of 40 percent or more minority race concentration were used to obtain the needed number. The more targeted sampling allowed us to obtain the required number of whites and blacks without extraordinary costs. However, this method does over sample minorities who live among 40 percent or more minorities. Samples, drawn by Survey Sampling, Inc. of Fairfield, CT, used a random digit dialing procedure to which the survey center applied a screen for registered voters. Table A.1 describes the percentages of black and white (non-black) respondents from the base sample and oversample in each city.

Response Rate #3 in AAPOR's Standard Definitions: Final Disposition of Case Codes and Outcome Rates for RDD Telephone Surveys and In-Person Household Surveys was utilized, and the response rates in the four cities were as follows: New Orleans had a 63 percent response rate; Chicago, 55 percent; Charlotte, 58 percent; and Detroit, 53 percent. These response rates are respectable considering that half of the sample is urban African American, a largely low-income group that is more difficult to include in telephone surveys.

Interviewers for all four surveys were university students. Students conducted the interviews from a central phone bank with constant supervision by a graduate student. The survey center used a CATI (Computer Assisted Telephone Interviewing) system in order to manage samples, and as many as fifteen attempts were made to reach respondents. The final number of blacks and whites interviewed in each city is as follows: New Orleans, blacks—253, whites—252; Detroit, blacks—282, whites—250; Charlotte, blacks—256, whites—273; Chicago, blacks—262, whites—250.

Question Wording

Mayoral Approval
In general, do you approve or disapprove of the job Mayor XX is doing? (PAUSE) Is that strongly or not very strongly?

Services
I would like to ask you about government and government services in the city. Is each of the following aspects of government very good, good, fair, poor or very poor? Overall level of government services, drainage and flood control, control of abandoned housing, health services, services for the poor, quality of housing, control of litter and trash, parks and recreation, control of pollution.

Police
I would like to ask you about government and government services in the city. Is each of the following aspects of government very good, good, fair, poor or very poor? Police Protection.

How would you rate the XX police on the following? The ability of the XX police to respond quickly to calls for help and assistance? The ability of the police to find the criminals after a crime has been committed? Being courteous, helpful and friendly? Avoiding the use of unnecessary or excessive force?

Safety
In general, how safe do you feel from crime walking in your neighborhood during the day? (Very Safe, Safe, Not Very Safe, Not at all Safe). During the night? Walking downtown at night?

Crime
Turning to crime and safety, would you say that the amount of crime in XX has increased, decreased, or remained about the same over the last several years?

Economy

Now I'd like to ask you some questions about the economy in XX. Is each of the following very good, good, fair, poor or very poor? Opportunities for employment? Likelihood of new jobs and industry coming into the city? Likelihood of your family increasing its income in the next several years?

Transportation

Now I would like to ask you about transportation in XX. Are each of the following very good, good, fair, poor or very poor? Conditions of your local streets and roads? Availability of public transportation within the city? Control of traffic congestion?

General Evaluations

Thinking back over the last five years, would you say that XX has become a better or worse place to live, or hasn't there been any change?

And thinking ahead over the next five years, do you think that XX will become a better or worse place to live, or won't there be much of a change?

Schools

Now thinking about education, how would you rate the quality of public schools in XX, very good, good, fair, poor or very poor?

Symbolic Racism

1) Over the past few years blacks have gotten less than they deserve (agree strongly to disagree strongly).
2) Irish, Italians, Jews and other minorities overcame prejudice and worked their way up. Blacks should do the same without any special favors.
3) In past studies, we have asked people why they think white people seem to get more of the good things in life in America—such as better jobs and more money than black people do. These are some of the reasons given by both blacks and whites. It's really just a matter of some people not trying hard enough. If blacks would only try harder they could be just as well off as whites.
4) Generations of slavery and discrimination have created conditions that make it difficult for blacks to work their way out of the lower class.

Group Conflict

1) More good jobs for blacks means fewer good jobs for members of other groups (agree strongly to disagree strongly).
2) The more influence blacks have in local politics the less influence members of other groups will have in politics.
3) As more good housing and neighborhoods go to blacks, the fewer good houses and neighborhoods there will be for members of other groups.
4) Many blacks have been trying to get ahead at the expense of other groups.

Black Linked Fate
Do you think what happens generally to black people in this country will have something to do with what happens in your life? (if Yes) Will it affect you a lot, some, or not very much?

Black Solidarity
How important is it for blacks to vote for black candidates when they run for office—extremely important, very important or only somewhat important? (not very important: volunteered). To participate in black-only organizations whenever possible? To have control over the government in mostly black communities? To have control over the economy in mostly black communities?

Black Neighborhood
How would you describe your neighborhood racially—almost all white, mostly white, about an equal number of blacks and whites, mostly black, or almost all black?

Table A.1 Composition of Final Samples

		White	*Black*
New Orleans	Cross-section	87%	99%
	Oversample	13	1
	N	(252)	(253)
Detroit	Cross-section	28%	84%
	Oversample	72	16
	N	(250)	(282)
Charlotte	Cross-section	92%	42%
	Oversample	8	58
	N	(273)	(256)
Chicago	Cross-section	92%	50%
	Oversample	8	50
	N	(250)	(262)

Table A.2 Race and Latino Ethnic Composition of Adult Populations (18+) of Four Cities (1990 Census)

	New Orleans	*Detroit*	*Charlotte*	*Chicago*
Black	56.3%	73.1%	28.6%	36.1%
White	40.7	24.4	68.9	50.0
Other	3.0	2.5	2.5	13.9
Latino Ethnicity (All Races)	3.6	2.4	1.3	16.7

Table A.3 Full Models for Table 5.3

Dependent Variables						
Independent Variables	*Safety*	*Economy*	*Transportation*	*Crime Dec.*	*General Evaluation*	*Schools*
Race	0.03[a]	—	—	—	—	0.54***
Female	-0.08***	—	0.02*	-0.42***	—	—
Age	-0.02***	-0.02***	—	—	-0.09**	0.12***
Income	0.02***	0.02***	—	0.06[a]	0.07*	—
Education	0.01*	0.01**	—	—	—	-0.18***
Black Interviewer	—	—	—	—	—	—
Conservative Ideology	-0.02*	—	—	-0.21**	-0.16*	—
Black City	-0.05***	-0.14***	-0.09***	0.56***	—	-1.26***
Black Neighborhood	-0.12***	-0.12***	-0.05*	—	-0.46*	-0.42*
Adj R^2 or BIC'	0.10	0.20	0.07	-54.02	30.21	-184.64
N	1724	1724	1724	1724	1724	1724

[a] $p < 0.10$
* $p < 0.05$
** $p < 0.01$
*** $p < 0.001$

Table A.4 Full Models of Mayoral Approval (ordered logit)

Y = Mayoral Approval	*New Orleans*	*Detroit*	*Charlotte*	*Chicago*
Race (Black)	1.21***	-0.77**	—	—
Services	3.66***	4.03***	3.43**	1.93*
Police	1.74**	1.50*	3.09***	1.86**
Schools	—	0.72[a]	1.22*	—
Economy	—	1.56**	—	2.17***
Safety	—	—	—	0.82[a]
Crime Decreasing	—	0.45[a]	—	—
Transportation	—	—	—	1.70*
Black Neighborhood	—	—	—	—
Gender	—	—	—	—
Age	—	—	—	—
Income	—	—	—	—
Education	—	—	—	-0.38***
Black Interviewer	0.41[a]	-0.58*	—	—
Ideology (Cons.)	—	—	0.35*	—
Party ID (Rep.)	-0.38*	—	—	-0.32[a]
Threshold 1	1.03	1.68	2.37	1.22
Threshold 2	1.79	2.43	3.38	2.27
Threshold 3	3.57	4.47	5.95	4.35
N	398	416	369	410
Cragg & Uhler's R^2	0.34	0.34	0.31	0.37
BIC'	-51.26	-61.18	-25.12	-71.21

* $p < 0.05$
** $p < 0.01$
*** $p < 0.001$
[a] $p < 0.10$

Note: dashes indicate insignificant ologit coefficients.

References

Adler, J. S. 2001. Introduction. In *African American mayors: Race, politics, and the American city*, eds. D. R. Colburn and J. S. Adler, 1–22. Urbana: University of Illinois Press.

Albritton, R. B., G. Amedee, K. Grenell, and D.-T. Veal. 1996. Deracialization and the new black politics. In *Race, politics, and governance in the United States*, ed. H. L. Perry, 79–102. Gainesville: University Press of Florida.

Ardrey, S. C., and W. E. Nelson. 1990. The maturation of black political power: The case of Cleveland. *PS: Political Science and Politics* (June): 148–51.

Baldassare, M. 2003. *PPIC statewide survey*. San Francisco: Public Policy Institute of California.

Banfield, E. 1961. *Big city politics*. New York: Free Press.

Barnes, C. W., Jr. 1994. Atlanta's post-civil rights political economy: Demobilization and economic dependency. Paper presented at the annual meeting of the Southern Political Science Association, Atlanta.

Bayor, R. H. 1996. *Race and the shaping of twentieth-century Atlanta*. Chapel Hill: University of North Carolina Press.

———. 2001. African American mayors and governance in Atlanta. In *African American mayors: Race, politics, and the American city*, eds. D. R. Colburn and J. S. Adler, 178–99. Urbana: University of Illinois Press.

Bergesen, A. 1980. Official violence during the Watts, Newark, and Detroit race riots of the 1960s. In *A political analysis of deviance*, ed. P. Lauderdale, 138–74. Minneapolis: University of Minnesota Press.

Biles, R. 1995. *Richard J. Daley: Politics, race, and the governing of Chicago*. DeKalb: Northern Illinois University Press.

———. 2001. Mayor David Dinkins and the politics of race in New York City. In *African American mayors: Race, politics, and the American city*, eds. D. R. Colburn and J. S. Adler, 130–52. Urbana: University of Illinois Press.

Bledsoe, T., S. Welch, L. Sigelman, and M. Combs. 1995. Residential context and racial solidarity among African Americans. *American Journal of Political Science* 39 (May): 434–58.

Bloch, P. B. 1974. *Equality of distribution of police services: A case study of Washington D.C.* Washington, DC: Urban Institute.

Blumer, H. 1958. Race prejudice as a sense of group position. In *Race relations: Problems and theory*, eds. J. Masouka and P. Valien, 217–27. Chapel Hill: University of North Carolina Press.

Bobo, J. 1975. *The New Orleans economy: Pro bono publico?* New Orleans: College of Business Administration, University of New Orleans.

Bobo, L. 1988a. Attitudes toward the black political movement: Trends, meaning and effects on racial policy preferences. *Social Psychology Quarterly* 51:287–302.

———. 1988b. Group conflict, prejudice and the paradox of racial attitudes. In *Eliminating racism: Profiles in controversy*, eds. P. Katz and D. A. Taylor, 85–114. New York: Plenum.

———. 2000. Race and beliefs about Affirmative Action: Assessing the effects of interests, group threat, ideology, and racism. In *Racialized politics: The debate about racism in America*, eds. D. O. Sears, J. Sidanius, and L. D. Bobo, 137–64. Chicago: University of Chicago Press.

Bobo, L., and F. D. Gilliam, Jr. 1990. Race, sociopolitical participation, and black empowerment. *American Political Science Review* 84 (June): 377–93.

———. 1997. Race, public opinion, and the social sphere. *Public Opinion Quarterly* 61 (Spring): 1–15.

Bobo, L. D., and V. L. Hutchings. 1996. Perceptions of racial group competition: Extending Blumer's Theory of Group Position to a multiracial social context. *American Sociological Review* 61:951–72.

Brody, R. A. 1991. *Assessing the president: The media, elite opinion, and public support*. Stanford, CA: Stanford University Press.

Brown, E. L. 1944. *Why race riots? Lessons from Detroit*. New York: Public Affairs Committee.

Brown, K., and P. B. Coulter. 1983. Subjective and objective measures of police performance. *Public Administration Review* 43:50–58.

Browning, R. P., D. R Marshall, and D. H. Tabb. 1984. *Protest is not enough*. Berkeley: University of California Press.

———. 1990. *Racial politics in American cities*. New York: Longman.

———. 2003. *Racial politics in American cities*. 3rd ed. New York: Longman.

Bureau of Justice Statistics. 2000. *Sourcebook of criminal justice statistics 1999*. NCJ-183727. Washington, DC: Office of Justice Programs, U.S. Department of Justice.

———. 2003. *Criminal victimization in the United States, 2002 statistical tables*. Washington, DC: Office of Justice Programs, U.S. Department of Justice.

Campbell, A., and H. Schuman. 1968. *Racial attitudes in fifteen American cities*. Ann Arbor, MI: Survey Research Center, Institute for Social Research.

Campbell-Rock, C. C. 2004. The legacy of New Orleans' African-American mayors. *The New Orleans Tribune* 19, no. 12 (December / January): 10–11.

Canon, D. T. 1999. *Race, redistricting, and representation: The unintended consequences of black majority districts*. Chicago: University of Chicago Press.

Carmines, E. G., and J. A. Stimson. 1989. *Issue evolution: Race and the transformation of American politics*. Princeton: Princeton University Press.

Carpenter, B. 2005. Takeover as a reform strategy. *School Reform News*, The Heartland Institute, February 21. Available at http://www.heartland.org/Article.cfm?artId=16297.

Chernick, J., B. Indik, and G. Sternlieb. 1967. *New Jersey population and labor force characteristics*. Newark, NJ: Graduate School of Business, Rutgers University.

Chesler, M., M. Peet, and T. Sevig. 2003. Blinded by whiteness: The development of white college students' racial awareness. In *White out: The continuing significance of racism*, eds. A. Doane and E. Bonilla-Silva, 215–231. New York: Routledge.

Chicago Urban League Department of Research and Planning. 1991. *The geography of opportunity: The status of African Americans in the Chicago area economy.* Washington, DC: Brookings Institution Press.

Chubb, J. E. 1988. Institutions, the economy and the dynamics of state elections. *American Political Science Review* 82 (March): 133–154.

Citrin, J., D. P. Green, and D. O. Sears. 1990. White candidates reactions to black candidates: When does race matter?" *Public Opinion Quarterly* 54 (Spring): 74–96.

Cohen, A., and E. Taylor. 2000. *American pharaoh: Mayor Richard J. Daley: His battle or Chicago and the nation.* Boston: Little, Brown, and Company.

Colburn, D. R. 2001. Running for office: African-American mayors from 1967 to 1996. In *African American mayors: Race, politics, and the American city*, eds. D. R. Colburn and J. S. Adler, 23–56. Urbana: University of Illinois Press.

Colburn, D., and J. Adler. 2001. *African-American mayors: Race, politics and the American city.*Chicago: University of Illinois Press.

Cunningham, L. 1990. The mayor's race: Two kinds of leaders. *The Times-Picayune*, January 12, sec. A-4.

Dalton, R. 1980. Reassessing parental socialization: Indicator unreliability versus generational transfer. *American Political Science Review* 74 (June): 421–31.

Davis, D. W., and B. D. Silver. 2003. Stereotype threat and race of interviewer effects in a survey on political knowledge. *American Journal of Political Science* 47 (1): 33–45.

Dawson, M. C. 1994. *Behind the mule: Race and class in African-American politics.* Princeton: Princeton University Press.

Danziger, S. H., and R. Farley. 2000. *Detroit divide.* New York: Russell Sage Foundation.

Decker, S. 1981. Citizen attitudes toward the police: A review of past findings and suggestions for future policy. *Journal of Political Science and Administration* 9 (1): 80–87.

Doane, W. 2003. Rethinking whiteness studies. In *White out: The continuing significance of racism*, eds. A. Doane and E. Bonilla-Silva, 3–19. New York: Routledge.

Dzwonkowski, R. 2001. The mayor of more than Detroit. *Detroit Free Press*, September, 21, 2E.

Edelman, M. 1964. *The symbolic uses of politics.* Urbana: University of Illinois Press.

———. 1971. *Politics as symbolic action.* Chicago: Markham.

———. 1975. *Political language.* New York: Academic Press.

Edsall, T., and M. Edsall. 1991. *Chain reaction: The impact of race, rights, and taxes on American politics.* New York: Norton.

Edwards, G. C., III, W. Mitchell, and R. Welch. 1995. Explaining presidential approval: The significance of issue salience. *American Journal of Political Science* 39 (February): 108–134.

Eisinger, P. K. 1980. *Politics of displacement: Racial and ethnic transition in three American cities.* New York: Academic Press.

________ 1982. Black employment in municipal jobs: The impact of black political power. *American Political Science Review* 76 (June): 380–92.

Elder, C. D., and R. W. Cobb. 1983. *The political uses of symbols*. White Plains, NY: Longman.

Emig, A. G., M. B. Hesse, and S. H. Fisher, III. 1996. Black-white differences in political efficacy, trust, and sociopolitical participation: A critique of the empowerment hypothesis. *Urban Affairs Review* 32 (November): 264–276.

Engstrom, R. L., and W. Kirkland. 1995. The 1994 New Orleans mayoral election: Racial divisions continue. *Urban News* 9:6–9.

Entman, R. M. 1992a. Representing order: Crime, law and justice in the news media. *American Journal of Sociology* 97 (May): 1776—79.

_________. 1992b. Blacks in the news: Television, modern racism and cultural change (Special emphasis: America in a visual century). *Journalism Quarterly* 69 (Summer): 341–62.

Evans, M. 1931. *A study of the state government of Louisiana*. Baton Rouge: Louisiana State University Press.

Farley, R., S. Danziger, and H. J. Holzer. 2000. *Detroit divided*. New York: Russell Sage Foundation.

Fairclough, A. 1995. *Race & democracy: The civil rights struggle in Louisiana 1915–1972*. Athens: University of Georgia Press.

Finkel, S. E., T. M. Guterbock, and M. J. Borg. 1999. Race of interviewer effects in a preelection poll: Virginia 1999. *Public Opinion Quarterly* 55 (3): 313–30.

Flessner, D. 2001. Voting along racial lines. *Chattanooga Times Free Press*, March 8.

Fogelson, R. M. 1968. From resentment to confrontation: The police, the negroes, and the outbreak of the nineteen-sixties riots. *Political Science Quarterly* 83:217–47.

Fossett, M. A., and K. J. Kiecolt. 1989. The relative size of minority populations and white racial attitudes. *Social Science Quarterly* 70 (December): 820–35.

Friesema, P. H. 1969. Black control of central cities: The hollow prize. *American Institute of Planners Journal* 35:75–79.

Funk, C. 1999. Bringing the candidate into models of candidate evaluation. *Journal of Politics* 61:700–720.

Furstenberg, F. F., and C. F. Wellford. 1973. Calling the police: The evaluation of police service. *Law and Society Review* 7:393–406.

Gallagher, C. 2003. Playing the white ethnic card: Using ethnic identity to deny contemporary racism. In *White out: The continuing significance of racism*, eds. A. Doane and E. Bonilla-Silva, 145–58. New York: Routledge.

Gallup–Black, A. 2003. Changing of the guard: Mayors, race, engagement, and efficacy. Paper presented at the annual conference of the American Association of Public Opinion Research, Nashville, TN.

Gilliam, F. D., Jr., and K. M. Kaufman. 1998. Is there an empowerment life cycle? *Urban Affairs Review* 33:741–66.

Giles, M. W. 1977. Percent black and racial hostility: An old assumption reexamined." *Social Science Quarterly* 58:412–17.

Giles, M. W., and M. A. Buckner. 1993. David Duke and black threat: An old hypothesis revisited. *Journal of Politics* 55 (August): 702–13.

Giles, M., and K. Hertz. 1994. Racial threat and partisan identification. *American Political Science Review* 88 (June): 317–26.

Glaser, J. M. 1994. Back to the black belt: Racial environment and white racial attitudes in the south." *Journal of Politics* 56 (February): 21–41.

Gray, J. 1973. Jackson, Williams are "Racists." *Atlanta Constitution*, October 8.

Green, D. P., D. Z. Strolovitch, and J. S. Wong. 1998. Defended neighborhoods, integration, and racially motivated crime. *American Journal of Sociology* 104 (September): 372–403.

Greenfield, L. A., P. A. Lanagan and S. K. Smith. 1997. Police use of force: Collection of national data. NJC-165040. Washington DC: U.S. Department of Justice, Office of Justice Programs, Bureau of Justice Statistics.

Grimshaw, W. J. 1982. The Daley legacy: A declining politics of party, race and public unions." In *After daley: Chicago politics in transition*, eds. S. Gove and L. Masotti, 57–87. Urbana: University of Illinois Press.

Gurin, P., S. Hatchett, and J. S. Jackson. 1989. *Hope and independence: Blacks' response to electoral and party politics*. New York: Russell Sage Foundation.

Gurwitt, R. 2000. In recovery, launching an urban comeback. *Governing Magazine Online*. Available at http://www.governing.com/poy/2000/oArcher.htm.

Hahn, H., D. Klingman, and H. Pachon. 1976. Cleavages, coalitions, and the black candidate: The Los Angeles mayoralty elections of 1969 and 1973. *Western Political Quarterly* 29 (December): 507–20.

Hajnal, Z. L. 2001. White residents, black incumbents, and a declining racial divide. *American Political Science Review* 95 (September): 603–17.

———. 2004. Uncertainty, experience with black representation, and the white vote. In *Everything but death and taxes: Uncertainty and the study of American politics*, ed. B. C. Burden, 213–43. Cambridge: Cambridge University Press.

Hanchett, T. W. 1998. *Sorting out the New South city*. Chapel Hill: University of North Carolina Press.

Haas, E. F. 1972. The illusion of reform: DeLesseps S. Morrison and New Orleans politics, 1946–1961. PhD diss., University of Maryland.

———. 1974. *DeLesseps S. Morrison and the image of reform: New Orleans politics, 1946–1961*. Baton Rouge: Louisiana State University Press.

Heatherington, M. J., and M. Nelson. 2003. Anatomy of a rally effect: George W. Bush and the war on terrorism. *PS: Political Science and Politics* 36 (January): 37–50.

Hendrickson, W. W., ed. 1991. *Detroit perspectives, crossroads and turning points*. Detroit: Wayne State University Press.

Herman, M. 2002. *Ethnic succession and urban unrest in Newark and Detroit during the summer of 1967*. Newark, NJ: Cornwall Center Publication Series.

Hibbing, J. R., and E. Theiss-Morse. 1998. The media's role in public negativity toward Congress: Distinguishing emotional reactions and cognitive evaluations. *American Journal of Political Science* 42:475–98.

Hibbs. D. A., Jr., R. D. Rivers, and N. Vasilatos. 1982. The dynamics of political support for American presidents among occupational and partisan groups. *American Journal of Political Science* 26 (May): 312–32.

Hirsch, A. R. 1992. Simply a matter of black and white: The transformation of race and politics in twentieth-century New Orleans. In *Creole New Orleans: Race and Americanization*, eds. A. R. Hirsch and J. Logsdon, 262–319. Baton Rouge: Louisiana State University Press.

———. 2001. Harold and Dutch revisited: A comparative look at the first black mayors of Chicago and New Orleans. In *African American mayors: Race, politics, and the American city*, eds. D. R. Colburn and J. S. Adler, 107–29. Urbana: University of Illinois Press.

Hochschild, J. 1995. *Facing up to the American dream: Race, class, and the soul of a nation*. Princeton: Princeton University Press.

Howell, S. E. 1988–2004. New Orleans quality of life surveys. New Orleans Survey Research Center, University of New Orleans.

Howell, S. E., and W. McLean. 2001. Performance models and minority mayors. *Public Opinion Quarterly* 65:321–43.

Howell, S. E. and J. M. Vanderleeuw. 1990. Economic effects on state governors. *American Politics Quarterly* 18:158–68.

Howell, S. E., H. L. Perry, and M. Vile. 2004. Black cities / white cities: Evaluating the police. *Political Behavior* 26 (March): 45–68.

Humphrey, S. M.1994. Permanent interests: A history of African-American political organizations in New Orleans Louisiana 1940–1980. Master's thesis, Southern University—Baton Rouge Campus.

Illinois Advisory Committee to the U.S. Commission on Civil Rights. 1993. *Police protection on the African American community in Chicago*. U.S. Commission on Civil Rights.

Iyengar, S., and D. R. Kinder. 1987. *News that matters*. Chicago: University of Chicago Press.

Jacoby, T. 1998. *Someone else's house: Americas unfinished struggle for integration*. New York: Basic Books.

Jamieson, K. H. 1992. *Dirty politics: Deception, distraction and democracy*. New York: Oxford University Press.

Johnson, D. 2003. Justice or "just us"? Perceived racial bias in the criminal justice system. Paper presented at the annual conference of the American Association for Public Opinion Research, Nashville, TN.

Joint Center for Political and Economic Studies. 1977. *Joint center data bank: Profiles of black mayors in America*. Washington, DC. Available at http://www.jointcenter.org/DB/detail.htm.

Katz, A. 1982. Candidates tell ideas to students. *The Time-Picayune*, January 7, sec. 1, 26.

Keiser, R. A. 1997. *Subordination or empowerment? African-American leadership and the struggle for urban political power*. New York: Oxford University Press.

Kernell, S. 1978. Explaining presidential popularity. How ad hoc theorizing, misplaced emphasis, and insufficient care in measuring one's variables refuted common sense and led conventional wisdom down the path of anomalies. *American Political Science Review* 72 (June): 506–22.

Key, V. O. 1966. *The responsible electorate*. Cambridge, MA: Harvard University Press.

Kinder D. R., and T. Mendelberg. 2000. Individualism reconsidered. In *Racialized politics: The debate about racism in America*, eds. D. O. Sears, J. Sidanius, and L. Bobo. Chicago: University of Chicago Press, 44–74.

Kinder, D. R., and L. M. Sanders. 1996. *Divided by color*. Chicago: University of Chicago Press.

Kinder, D. R., and D. O. Sears. 1981. Prejudice and politics: Symbolic racism versus racial threats to the good life. *Journal of Personality and Social Psychology* 40 (3): 414–31.

King, G., R. O. Keohane, and S. Verba. 1994. *Designing social inquiry*. Princeton: Princeton University Press.

King, W. 1977. New Orleans mayoral vote: A black vs. white. *New York Times*, November 12, 8.

Kleppner, P. 1985. *Chicago divided: The making of a black mayor*. De Kalb: Northern Illinois Press.

Kraus, N., and T. Swanstrom. 2001. Minority mayors and the hollow-prize problem. *PS: Political Science and Politics* 34 (March): 99–105.

Lane, J. B. Black political power and its limits: Gary Mayor Richard G. Hatcher's administration, 1968–87. In *African American mayors: Race, politics, and the American city*, eds. D. R. Colburn and J. S. Adler, 57–79. Urbana: University of Illinois Press.

Lerner, M. J., and D. T. Miller. 1978. Just world research and the attribution process. *Psychological Bulletin* 85:1030–51.

Levine, D. A. 1976. *Internal combustion: The races in Detroit 1915–1926*. Westport, CT: Greenwood Press.

Linthicum, T. 1973. Massell's strategy—Play on white fears. *Atlanta Constitution*, October 8.

Liu, B. 2005. Whites as a minority and the new biracial coalition in New Orleans and Memphis. *Political Science* 39:69–76.

Long, J. S. 1997. *Regression models for categorical and limited dependent variables*. Vol. 7, *Advanced quantitative techniques in the social sciences*. Thousand Oaks, CA: Sage.

Long, J. S., and J. Freese. 2003. *Regression models for categorical dependent variables using stata*. College Station, TX: Stata.

Lorge, I., and C. C. Curtiss. 1936. Prestige, suggestion, and attitudes. *Journal of Social Psychology* 7:386–402.

Lublin, D., and D. S. Voss. 2000. Racial redistricting and realignment in southern state legislatures. *American Journal of Political Science* 44 (October): 792–810.

MacKuen, M. B. 1983. Political drama, economic conditions, and the dynamics of presidential popularity. *American Journal of Political Science* 27 (May): 165–92.

MacKuen, M. B., R. S. Erikson, and J. A. Stimson. 1992. Peasants or bankers? The American electorate and the U.S. economy. *American Political Science Review* 86 (September): 597–611.

Marschall, M. 2005. Minority incorporation and local school boards. In *Besieged: School boards and the future of education politics*, ed. W. Howell, 173–98. Brookings Institution Press.

Marschall, M., and A. Ruhil 2007. Substantive symbols: The attitudinal dimension of black political incorporation in local government. *American Journal of Political Science* 51 (January): 17–33.

Marschall, M., and P. Shah. 2005. "Keeping policy churn off the agenda: Urban education and civic capacity. *Policy Studies Journal* 33:161–80.

Markus, G. B. 1992. The impact of personal and national economic conditions on presidential voting, 1956–1988. *American Journal of Political Science* 36:829–34.

McCormick, J. P., and C. E. Jones. 1993. The conceptualization of deracialization: Thinking through the dilemma." In *Dilemmas of black politics: Issues of leadership and strategy*, ed. G. A. Persons, 66–84. New York: Harper Collins College Publishers.

McClain, P. D. 1993. The changing dynamics of urban politics: Black and Hispanic municipal employment—Is there competition?" *Journal of Politics* 55 (May): 399–414.

McConahay, J. B., and J. C. Hough. 1976. Symbolic racism. *Journal of Social Issues* 32:23–45.

McDermott, M. L.1998. Race and gender cues in low-information elections. *Political Research Quarterly* 51 (December): 895–918.

McGuire Research Services. 2000. Public satisfaction survey: New York City police. Prepared for the NYC Council, August. Available at http://www.council.nyc.ny.us/pdf.

———. 2001. Public satisfaction survey: New York City police. Prepared for the NYC Council, August. Available at http://www.council.nyc.ny.us/pdf.

Meier, K., and R. England. 1984. Black representation and educational policy: Are they related? *American Political Science Review* 78:392–403.

Mendelberg, T. 2001. *The race card: Campaign strategy, implicit messages, and the norm of equality*. Princeton: Princeton University Press.

Merelman, R. M. 1986. Domination, self-justification, and self-doubt: Some social-psychological considerations. *Journal of Politics* 48 (May): 276–300.

Miller, A. H., and M. P. Wattenberg. 1985. Throwing the rascals out: Policy and performance evaluations of presidential candidates, 1952–1980. *American Political Science Review* 79 (June): 359–72.

Miller, W. E., and J. M. Shanks. 1996. *The new American voter*. Cambridge, MA: Harvard University Press.

Mladenka, K. R. 1989. Blacks and Hispanics in urban politics. *American Political Science Review* 83 (March): 165–91.

Moesher, J., and C. Silver. 1994. Race, social stratification and politics. *Virginia Magazine of History and Biography* 102 (October): 519–50.

Mohai, P. 1990. Detroit area study: Community issues. Inter-University Consortium for Political and Social Research, University of Michigan.

Moore, L. N. 2001. Carl Stokes: Mayor of Cleveland. In *African American mayors: Race, politics, and the American city*, eds. D. R. Colburn and J. S. Adler, 80–106. Urbana: University of Illinois Press.

Montemurri, P. 2001. Evaluation of an area. *Detroit Free Press*, December 21.

Munoz, C., Jr., and C. Henry. 1986. Rainbow coalitions in four big cities: San Antonio, Denver, Chicago and Philadelphia. *PS* 19 (Summer): 598–609.

Mutz, D. 1994. Contextualizing personal experience: The role of mass media. *Journal of Politics* 56:689–714.

Muzzio, D., and G. Van Ryzin. 2000. Satisfaction with New York City services: Report to the New York City Council New York City Council. Available at http://www.council.nyc.ny.us/pdf_files/reports/ssnycs.pdf.

———. 2001. Satisfaction with New York City services: Report to the New York City Council. New York City Council. Available at http://www.council.nyc.ny.us/pdf_files/reports/citysvcs.pdf.

Nadeau, R., and M. S. Lewis-Beck. 2001. National economic voting in U.S. presidential elections. *Journal of Politics* 63 (January): 159–81.

Nadeau, R., R. G. Niemi, D. P. Fan, and T. Amato. 1999. Elite economic forecasts, economic news, mass economic judgments, and presidential approval. *Journal of Politics* 61 (February): 109–35.

National Center for Victims of Crime. 2004. *Victimization by race/ethnicity*. Available at http://www.ncvc.org/ncvc/main.aspx?dbName=DocumentViewer&DocumentID=38722.

Nelson, W. 1990. Black mayoral leadership. *National Political Science Review* 2:188–95.

Nelson, W. E., Jr., and P. J. Meranto. 1977. *Electing black mayors.* Columbus: Ohio State University Press.

Niemi, R. G., and H. Weisberg. 2001. What determines vote? In *Controversies in voting behavior.* 4th ed., eds. R. G. Niemi and H. Weisberg, 180–99. Washington, DC: Congressional Quarterly Press.

Niemi, R. G., H. W. Stanley, and R. J. Vogel. 1995. State economies and state taxes: Do voters hold governors accountable? *American Journal of Political Science* 39 (November): 936–57.

Norpoth, H. 1996. Presidents and the prospective voter. *Journal of Politics* 58 (August): 776–92.

Ohio State University Center for Survey Research. 2002. *Report to the city of Columbus 2002 citizen satisfaction survey.* Ohio State University Center for Survey Research. Available at http://columbus.gov/2002%20citizen/2002_Col_satisfact_rpt_pt_total.pdf.

Olsen, M. E. 1970. Social and political participation of blacks. *American Sociological Review* 35:682–97.

Orey, B. d'A. 1999. Deracialization, racialization, or something in between? The making of a black mayor in Jackson, Mississippi." PhD diss., University of New Orleans.

Osgood, C. E., and P. H. Tannenbaum. 1955. The principle of congruity and the prediction of attitude change. *Psychological Review* 62:42–55.

Ostrom, C. W., Jr., and D. M. Simon. 1985. Promise and performance: A dynamic model of presidential popularity. *American Political Science Review* 79 (June): 334–58.

Parr, J. 1998. *Boundary crossers: Case studies of how ten of America's metropolitan regions work.* University of Maryland Academy of Leadership. Available at http://www.academy.umd.edu/publications/Boundary/CaseStudies/besdetroit.htm.

Parker, H. R. 2001. Tom Bradley and the politics of race. In *African American mayors: Race, politics, and the American city*, eds. D. R. Colburn and J. S. Adler, 153–77. Urbana: University of Illinois Press.

Parks, R. B. 1984. Linking objective and subjective measures of performance. *Public Administration Review* 44:118–27.

Peffley, M., T. Shields, and B. Williams. 1996. The intersection of race and crime in television news stories: An experimental study. *Political Communication* 13 (July–September): 309–28.

Peltzman, S. 1987. Economic conditions and gubernatorial elections. *American Economic Review* 77:293–97.

Perry, H. L. 1990. Black politics and mayoral leadership in Birmingham and New Orleans. *National Political Science Review* 2 (April): 154–60.

———. 1996. An analysis of major themes in the concept of deracialization. In *Race, politics and governance in the United States*, ed. H. L. Perry, 1–11. Gainesville: University Press of Florida.

———. 2000. Mayor Richard Arrington, Jr. and police community relations in Birmingham, Alabama. In *Governing middle-sized cities: Studies in mayoral leadership*, eds. J. R. Bowers and W. C. Rich, 103–18. Boulder, CO: Lynne Rienner.

———. 2003. The evolution and impact of biracial coalitions and black mayors in Birmingham and New Orleans. In *Racial politics in American cities*. 3rd ed., eds. R. P. Browning, D. R. Marshall, and D. H. Tabb, 227–54. White Plains, NY: Longman.

Perry, H. L., and A. Stokes. 1987. Politics and power in the sunbelt: Mayor morial of New Orleans. In *The new black politics: The search for political power*, eds. M. B. Preston, L. Henderson, and P. Puryear, 222–55. New York: Longman.

Popkin, N. S. 1981. Mayors and administrators of the city of New Orleans, 1946–1980. Document prepared for the Chief Administrative Office, City of New Orleans, June.

Preston, B. M. 1990. Symposium—Big city black mayors: Have they made a difference? *National Political Science Review* 2:129–95.

Przeworski, A, and H. Teune. 2001. *The logic of comparative social inquiry*. New York: John Wiley.

Rafferty, A. E. 1996. Bayesian model selection in social research. In *Sociological methodology*. Vol. 26, ed. P. V. Marsden, 111–63. Oxford: Basil Blackwell.

Reed, A. 1988. The black urban regime: Structural origins and constraints. *Comparative urban research* 1:139–89.

Reeves, K. 1997. *Voting hopes or fears? White voters, black candidates, and racial policies in America*. Oxford: Oxford University Press.

Reiser, L. 2003. Understanding the state takeover of Philadelphia's schools. *Philadelphia Public School Notebook*, Summer. Available at http://www.thenotebook.org/editions/2003/summer/understanding.htm.

Rich, W. 1989. *Coleman Young and Detroit politics*. Detroit: Wayne State University Press.

———. 1991. From motor city to service hub. In *Big City Politics in Transition*, eds. H. V. Savitch and J. C. Thomas, 64–85. Newbury Park, CA: Sage.

Scarsborough, E. 2006. Interview with author. February 18.

Schexnider, A. J. 1982. Political moblilization in the south: The election of a black mayor in New Orleans. In *The new black politics: The search for political power*, eds. M. Preston, L. Henderson, Jr., and P. Puryear, 221–38. White Plains, NY: Longman.

———. 1989. *Coleman Young and Detroit politics: From social activist to power broker*. Detroit: Wayne State University Press.

Scott, J. 2001. Race still tend to live apart in New York, census shows. *New York Times*, March 23, final edition.

Sears, D. O. 1988. Symbolic racism. In *Eliminating racism: Profiles in contoversy*, eds. P. A. Katz and D. A. Taylor, 53–84. New York: Plenum Press.

Sears, D. O., and D. R. Kinder. 1971. Racial tensions and voting in Los Angeles. In *Los Angeles: Viability and prospects for metropolitan leadership*, ed. W. Z. Hirsch, 51–88. New York: Praeger.

Sears, D. O., C. van Laar, M. Carrillo, and R. Kosterman. 1997. Is it really racism: The origins of white Americans' opposition to race-targeted policies. *Public Opinion Quarterly* 61 (Spring): 16–42.

Shingles, R. D. 1981. Black consciousness and political participation: The missing link. *American Political Science Review* 75:76–91.

Sidanius, J. 1993. The psychology of group conflict and the dynamics of oppression: A social dominance perspective. In *Explorations in political psychology*, eds. S. Iyengar and W. J. McGuire, 183–219. Durham, NC: Duke University Press.

Sidanius, J., and F. Pratto. 1999. *Social dominance: An intergroup theory of social hierarchy and oppression*. New York: Cambridge University Press.

Sidanius, J., P. Singh, J. J. Hetts, and C. Federico. 2000. It's not affirmative action, it's the blacks. In *Racialized politics: The debate about racism in America*, eds. D. Sears, J. Sidanius, and L. D. Bobo, 191–236. Chicago: University of Chicago Press.

Sigelman, L., S. Welch, T. Bledsoe, and M. Combs. 1997. Police brutality and public perceptions of racial discrimination: A tale of two beatings. *Political Research Quarterly* 50:777–91.

Singer, P. 2001. Racial divisions evident in mayoral voting. *Associated Press State and Local Wire*, Nov. 8, sec. State and Regional.

Singh, R. 1998. *The congressional black caucus: Racial politics in the U.S. Congress*. Thousand Oaks, CA: Sage.

Smith, D., N. Graham, and B. Adams. 1991. Minorities and the police: Attitudinal and behavioral questions. In *Race and criminal justice*, eds. M. Lynch and E. B. Patterson, 22–35. New York: Harrow and Heston.

Smith, P. E., and R. O. Hawkins. 1973. Victimization, types of citizen-police contacts, and attitudes toward the police. *Law and Society Review* 8:135–52.

Smith, S. S. 2004. *Boom for whom? Education, desegregation, and development in Charlotte*. New York: SUNY Press.

Smockl, J. 1999. "Swat go the cops: As police brutality increases, tactics raise questions. *Metro Times Detroit*, June 30. Available at http://www.metrotimes.com/19/39/Features/newSwap.htm.

Sniderman, P. M. 1993. The new look in public opinion research. In *The state of the discipline II*, ed. A. Finifter, 219–46. Washington, DC: American Political Science Association.

Sniderman, P. M., and T. Piazza. 2002. *Black pride and black prejudice*. Princeton: Princeton University Press.

Sniderman, P. M., T. Piazza, P. E. Tetlock, and A. Kendrick. 1991. The new racism. *American Journal of Political Science* 35:423–47.

Sonsenshein, R. 1986. Biracial coalition in Los Angeles. *PS* 19 (Summer): 582–90.

———. 1989. Can black candidates win statewide elections. *Political Science Quarterly* 105:219–41.

Steward, H. 2003. Whatever it takes to win, baby: A graphic lesson in the differences between U.S. and canadian elections. *The Toronto Sun*, March 2, sec. C.

Sugrue, T. 1996. *The origins of the urban crisis: Race and inequality in post-war Detroit*. Princeton: Princeton University Press.

Svoboda, C. J. 1995. Retrospective voting in gubernatorial elections: 1982 and 1986. *Political Research Quarterly* 48 (March): 135–50.

Tate, K. 2003. *Black faces in the mirror: African Americans and their representatives in the U.S. Congress*. Princeton: Princeton University Press.

Taylor, M. C. 1998. How white attitudes vary with the racial composition of local populations: Numbers count. *American Sociological Review* 63 (August): 512–35.

———. 2000. The significance of racial context. In *Racialized politics: The debate about racism in America*, eds. D. O. Sears, J. Sidanius, and L. D. Bobo, 118–36. Chicago: University of Chicago Press.

Taylor, T. J., K. B. Turner, F.-A. Esbensen, and L. T. Winfree, Jr. 2001. Coppin' an attitude: Attitudinal differences among juveniles toward police. *Journal of Criminal Justice* 29:295–305.

Terkildsen, N. 1993. When white voters evaluate black candidates: The processing implications of candidate skin color, prejudice, and self-monitoring. *American Journal of Political Science* 37 (November): 1032–53.

Thernstrom, A. 1987. *Whose votes count? Affirmative action and minority voting rights.* Cambridge: Harvard University Press.

Thomas, J. M. 1997. *Redevelopment and race: Planning a finer city in postwar Detroit.* Baltimore: Johns Hopkins University Press.

Thompson, H. A. 2001. Rethinking the collapse of postwar liberalism: The rise of mayor Coleman Young and the politics of race in Detroit. In *African American mayors: Race, politics, and the American city*, eds. D. R. Colburn and J. S. Adler, 227–48. Urbana: University of Illinois Press.

Travis, T.-M. C. 1986. Boston: The unfinished agenda. *PS* 19 (Summer): 610–17.

Tuch, S., and R. Weitzer. 1997. Racial differences in attitudes toward the police. *Public Opinion Quarterly* 61:642–63.

Turner, R. L. 1983. Discouraging election for progressives. *Boston Globe*, November 17, sec. Op-Ed.

University of North Carolina. J. Murrey Atkins Library. 1987. Harvey B. Gantt papers. *Mayoral campaigns (1983, 1985, 1987): Clippings and correspondence.* Charlotte: University of North Carolina.

United States Census Bureau. 2000. Available at http://www.census.gov.

Vanderleeuw, J. M. 1990. A city in transition: The impact of changing racial composition on voting behavior. *Social Science Quarterly* 71 (June): 326–38.

Van Ryzin, G. G., D. Muzzio, and S. Immerwahr. 2004. Explaining the race gap in satisfaction with urban services. *Urban Affairs Review* 39:613–32.

Verba, S., and N. H. Nie. 1972. *Participation in America.* New York: Harper and Row.

WABC TV/New York Daily News. 1989. Exit Poll. Ann Arbor, MI: InterUniversity Consortium for Political and Social Research.

Weisberg, H. F., and S. T. Mockabee. 1999. Attitudinal correlates of the 1996 presidential vote: The people reelect a president. In *Reelection 1996: How Americans voted*, eds. H. F. Weisberg and J. M. Box-Steffensmeier, 45–69. New York: Chatham House.

Waterman, R. W., H. C. Jenkins-Smith, and C. L. Silva. 1999. The expectations gap thesis: Public attitudes toward an incumbent president. *Journal of Politics* 61 (November): 944–66.

Welch, S., L. Sigelman, T. Bledsoe, and M. Combs. 2001. *Race and place: Residence and race relations in an American city.* Cambridge: Cambridge University Press.

Wong, K. K. and F. X. Shen. 2003. When mayors lead urban schools: Toward developing a framework to assess the effects of mayoral takeover of urban districts. Presented at School Board Politics Conference, Kennedy School of Government, Harvard University.

Index